The Story

of

Gumby

The Story

of

Gumby

Tracing the Family History to the 1700s

This book documents the Gumby family history in slavery through freedom in Virginia. Robert Carter III emancipated five-hundred slaves beginning in 1791. This manumission precedes Abraham Lincoln's 1865 emancipation of proclamation.

The Story of Gumby; Tracing the Family History to the 1700s
©2015 by Rosalind Gumby Bauchum

Jason E. Gines, PhD Editor
John Wesley Gumby, PhD Contributing Editor

For permission, contact the publisher; Purpose Publishing Ltd.,
1503 Main Street, #168, Grandview, Missouri (MO) 64030.

ISBN 978-0-9861063-0-9
Library of Congress: 2014960124

Inquiries may be addressed to the author, Rosalind Bauchum to;
storyofgumby@gmail.com
Website - www.storyofgumby.com

This book is available at special quantity discounts to use as
premiums in history, genealogy, and educational programs.

Front cover - *Eyre Crowe*, Slaves Waiting to Be Sold, *in Eyre
Crowe*, With Thackeray in America *(New York: C. Scribner's, 1893). In
Illustrated London News, 1856*

Image credits, Used with permission from Microsoft® software
Back cover photograph, *Norman Harris*

Acknowledgements

When my father, the late Harry L. Gumby became ill; I wanted dad to have the opportunity to read the history of our Gumby family. While discussing my plans with a friend, Jeanette Richard Miles, I told her I could write my family history in three days. The format, and my father's branch history was created in three days. However, additional research efforts extended the project's goal. A special thank you to Jeanette Miles for her inspiration, and supportive words in the development of this book. To my cousin, Anna E. Gumby Krishnappa, thank you for your valuable assistance in bridging the descendants of two brothers, John H. and Samuel D. Gumby; the sons of Nelson and Sarah Jane Gumby.

To my family; thank you for your encouragement as I developed this book. Special thanks to the Midwest Afro American Genealogy Interest Coalition (MAGIC), for their genealogy programs. I am grateful to Algy Giles Mason for introducing me to MAGIC. A special thank you to Reginald James, and to David W. Jackson, for reviewing and commenting on the book manuscript.

Thank you to Alexis Thomas MD, and Reginald Hall MD, for their help and guidance in supporting my health during the writing of this book. Thanks to Barbara Finnell RRT, Millicent McCain RN, and Mavis Perkins RN, for their helpful advice regarding my health status. Appreciation to Elisabeth Watkins, Reffiel Jones, Kathryn Flemming, Pearl Mitchell, Barbara Woodson, Bernice Thomas, Brenda Vann, Geneva Wilson, Julia Simpson, Rosalind Qualls, Patricia Bell, Rosemary Lowe, Shirley Walker, Jeraldine Todd, Brita L. Emerson, Joyce Sargent, Theresa Rutherford, Elinora Reynolds, Carlene Canady, and Carolyn Watkins for their thoughts, support, and prayers.

Thank you to the historic Morning Star M. B. Baptist Church of Kansas City MO, Dr. John Modest Miles, Senior Pastor, for supporting my endeavors.

Dedication

I am dedicating this book in the memory of my father and mother, Harry Lester and Doris Carroll Gumby, my grandparents, Harry Nelson Charles and Harriet Parker Gumby, and my great-grandparents John H. and Rachel Simms Gumby. This book is in memory of the Gumby slaves whom may be buried in the Nomini Hall slave plantation cemetery in Westmoreland County, Virginia.

This book is dedicated to my husband James W. A. Bauchum III, who observed my engagement in hours of researching and writing of the manuscript. Special dedication to our children, Jessica Ann Bauchum, and Stephanie Lorene Bauchum. In addition, this book is dedicated to my sisters; Brenda Gumby Gines (Bobby), Arvetta Gumby Prewitt (Thomas), and to my brother Harry Bernard Gumby III, (Juliet). Dedication to my uncle William L. Gumby, my aunts, Ethel, Edna, and Harriet Gumby, and to my nieces, nephews, and cousins. A special thank you and appreciation to Elder Dr. John Wesley Gumby Sr., for his support, information, and contributions to the book from his personal archives of the Gumby family history.

A very special appreciation and thank you to Dr. Linda M. Gumby Green for her prayers and inspiration.

In dedication and memory of our brother-friend Dewayne Holmes Sr., and to his wife, a special friend, Lillie D. Holmes.

A special dedication to the ancestors of the Gumby family, who were manumitted by Robert Carter III beginning in September of 1791.

Foreword

I am proud the author has delved into the research of our ancestry. This legacy of our ancestral beginnings, shows us the strength, perseverance, tenacity, and endurance these ancestors had in their journey from another continent to the British Americas in the 1600s.

The facts amassed in this book about the manumission of our ancestors during the 1700s, documents the compassion, humanity, and faith principles Robert Carter III held against slavery.

Rosalind Gumby Bauchum has returned to the archives of time to show her family as slaves in colonial Virginia. Although slavery is not a new topic in America, Rosalind documented her family's manumission occurring generations before other slaves were freed in 1865.

We are indebted to our sister, Rosalind Gumby Bauchum in the time and efforts placed in researching, collecting, assembling and writing of this history for the future generations of Gumby family members.

Brenda Gumby Gines

Contents

Part I From Africa to the Colonies 1

Chapter 1   Introduction..3

Chapter 3   Virginia Records 19

Chapter 4   Mount Holly Springs, PA...29

The Parsonage..31

The Gumby Escape to Freedom 32

Chapter 5   The Military 39

World War I 44

Part II The Gumby Descendants 51

Chapter 6   Professional Careers...53

Chapter 7   The Family Tree..69

Gumby, Owens 87

Gumby, Arter 89

Greason, Wilkerson, Curtis, James, Buck, Starkes 93

Manigault, Tumey, Milburn, Bass, Warder...94

Cuff, Spraglin 95

Wilkerson, Bird 96

Gumby-Murray 102

Gumby-Sanders...102

Chapter 8 Family Photographs 119

The Epilogue...127

Works Cited 131

Books by the Author 138

Part I
From Africa to the Colonies

Chapter 1
Introduction

"I drew off this morning for Dadda Gumby a list of his children, and their respective ages. He himself is 94 -- For this office, I had as many thanks, as I have had blessings before now from a Beggar for Sixpence."

"Thank you, thank you, thank you Master," was the language of the old Grey headed pair. Call on us at any time, you shall have eggs, apples, potatoes; you shall have everything we can get for you Master! In this torrent of expressions of gratitude, I was rung to breakfast; I bow'd to the venerable old Negroes, [1] thank'd them in my turn for their Offers, & left them." Wednesday 13. 1794 (Douthat) *– As recorded by Phillip Vickers Fithian.*

Tom Gumby, better known as Dadda Gumby, asked a teacher, Phillip V. Fithian to record his children and grandchildren in writing at Nomini Hall. Tom Gumby was unable to read, but he knew a written list of his children would become an important record of his family. The list of Tom Gumby's children is the first genealogy of the Gumby family. Phillip Fithian didn't include Dadda Gumby's list of children in his letters, or writings. Despite this omission, present day Gumby families have an ancestral connection with Thomas Gumby. Diaries, property tax lists, slave-owner letters and inventories, Census records document Tom Gumby's life.

What happened to the Gumby descendants of Dadda Gumby emancipated by Robert Carter III beginning in 1791? This research seeks to answer the questions and inquiries about Tom's family. One purpose for this book is to honor Tom Gumby as the forefather of the Gumby family in this country. This book shares insight of the Gumby family since Carter's emancipation.

In 1774, Nomini Hall had more than 600 slaves. Tom (Dadda) Gumby was the patriarch of slaves living at Nomini Hall and other plantations. Robert King Carter owned several large Virginia plantations including slaves. Fritz Kredel, a painter, drew Tom Gumby and his wife in a discussion with Phillip Vickers Fithian, a Nomini Hall tutor.

PHOTO 1. TOM AND KATE GUMBY

The Gumby Name

Gumby is a name with true gravitas because it has survived for several generations. More than one thousand persons surnamed Gumby live in the United States. Africans first arrived at Pointe Comfort Virginia in 1619 on the Portuguese ship the Sao Joao Bautista. (McCartney) These Africans may have come from Angola and other western African countries. Likewise, the name Gumby shows association with the African names of Gombe, Gomba, or Gombeh of Western Africa. Nineteenth-century books, references, and documents show African slaves named Gombe.

During the early 1800s, Gombe individuals were found on slave ships sailing to the Americas. British soldiers rescued the individuals and released them from slavery. The British recorded the names, origin, language, and tribes of these slaves. These African individuals with the names of Gombe/Gumbeh/Gumbe came from the North Congo, West Central Africa, and Angola (Luanda, Ambriz, and Novo Redondo). (Emory University, National Endowment for the Humanitites, W.E.B. Institute, Harvard University). The ships intercepted by the British were the Empressa, Jacuhy, Faceirinha, and the Dezoito de Outubro.

Gumby Africans may have come from the Ngombe (pronounced Gom-beh) tribe of Angola. Onstott's research identifies the Gombeh and Gombe tribes as originating from Angola (Onstott). Missionaries living in Africa wrote of a visit to the Ngombe Lisala tribe during forty years of service in the Congo (Randall).

During the 1600s, ships transported slaves from Africa to the Caribbean, and later to the British colonies. A transcript of a court record entry of September 20, 1659, noted the delivery of three slaves named Jacke, Lillely, and Gumby to the Arnett family at Christ Church Parrish, Barbados. (Arnett). The Gumby members were most likely from the West coast of Africa; the Cameroon, Ghana, Guinea, Ivory Coast, Nigeria or Sierra Leone (Barbados.Org).

Gumby surnamed slaves lived in the Commonwealth of Virginia in the early 1600s. A reference of the 1655 estate inventory of William Brocas lists a man named "Gumby" and a man called "Gratia" among slaves in Lancaster County, Virginia (Rutman). Eleanor Eltonhead Brocas, after the death of her husband inherited Gumby. Gumby was listed as fifty-years old in a family inventory and may have been born around 1605. (The Corotoman Slave Histories). [2] Eleanor Brocas later married John Carter of Corotoman, and Gumby became a part of the John Carter estate.

Martha Gamby/Gumby was born around 1675. Martha, of East Indian heritage was living in London, England when in 1701 or 1702 she made an agreement with Henry Conyers to travel to America to work as a servant. The following 1704 agreement was filed in the Stafford County, Virginia court as follows;

"Whereas I am now going to Virginia and whereas MARTHA GAMBY, an Indian, is contented to go with me as a hired servant, I do hereby promise and agree that the said MARTHA GAMBY does at any time within four years next coming desire to returne to England, that I will not only permit her freely to return to England I will also be assisting in her return to my power and pay for her passage back to England whenever she shall desire the same." Witnessed: Nich. Nichols, Sarah Bradshaw. (Information about Sarah Foote (32) Genealogy) (Genealogy; from Stafford County, Virginia Deeds and Wills, 1699-1709)

Paul Heinegg, author of "The Free African-Americans" website, refers to Martha Gamby as a possible beginning family link to John and Rachel Gumby. (Heinegg, Free African-Americans of North Carolina, Virginia and South Carolina; From the Colonial Period to 1820).

The author of this text does not substanciate the connection between Martha Gamby and the Gumby family as suggested by Paul Heinegg. The preference in this case, is to begin with the known descendants of Tom Gumby of Nomini Hall, Westmoreland, Virginia.

PHOTO 2 JOHN CARTER - PHOTO – WIKIPEDIA

Robert King Carter's 1733 inventory includes "Old Gumby," his wife Martha, and his son Jack as part of the plantation estate's inventory. During this time, the Gumby family lived on the Wolf House Quarter plantation, in Lancaster County, Virginia.

Robert King Carter's inventory identifies Tom Gumby and his wife Kate, with their daughter Mary, Dick, 13 years old, and a one-year old daughter named Martha. The family lived on the Home Plantation. (A. C. Society). Robert King Carter later amended his will and gave Mary to his son Charles; *"I give to my son Charles, my Mulatto girl Mary, Tom Gumbo's wife's daughter."* (Carter Papers).

Although information about Tom Gumby's father and mother, are unknown, Robert King Carter identified a man David, as Tom's brother. Carter wrote in his will; *"of my gift to my said son John, I give and devise unto my son Robert and to the heirs male, issue of his Body lawfully begotten as also the following negroe slaves (to wit) my negroe George the Cooper and his wife and Children, The two Negroes I have now bound out as apprentices to Wm. Garland Also the Negroe {sic} Boy that is an apprentice to George the Cooper, also my negroe {sic} boy David, Tom Gumby's Brother and likewise my Cook wench Press her husband Old Robin and her children."* (Jr.)

Information from letters and diary records show Robert King Carter seemed to trust his slave Tom. Carter sent Tom to deliver letters, deliver supplies, hunt, and fish around the plantation. The following excerpt is from Robert Carter's diary dated December 2, 1724.

"Tom Gumby fetcht {sic} Meal the 2d Decembr {sic} 9 bushels, 4 bushels, malt for Ale 1 bushel out of the new ` {sic} 4 Gumby carrys to Mill 6 bus[he] l[s] old wheat," December 4th 1724, *3 days ago, my Son Charles drew off out of my pip [e] of wine 30 dozen bottles 5 dozen more drew afterwards Henry Bell 8 shillings for ferriage signed*

Conditions 5 put up the Ale put out my [kiln] [sic] Captain Kenner here Gumby fetches flour."

Despite such trust, Tom, his family, and other slaves were viewed as property, and harshly treated. There were long days of hard labor, whippings, and mistreatment coupled with the lack of food, clothing and adequate shelter. Death was eminent for slaves who didn't comply with overseer demands. Robert King Carter in an October 10, 1727 letter instructed an overseer named Robert Jones to cut off the toes of a runaway slave. (Library of Virginia Archives). The photograph of an unknown man shows scars on his back. Slaves encountered multiple whippings, beatings, and abuse.

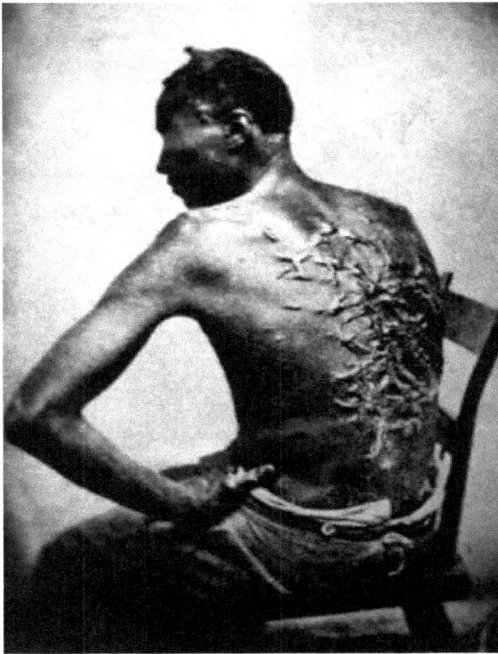

Library of Congress

Landon Carter, an uncle of Robert Carter III, believed slaves should be whipped. The Landon Carter slaves would routinely run away. Landon Carter had watchmen and would contact the militia to hunt for his runaways. Landon believed slaves needed harsh treatment to prevent certain behaviors. In addition, Carter said it was his right to punish his slaves as he pleased. (Hast).

Photo 3 Robert King Carter.

Source: Wikipedia

The record of the birth of a baby named "Gumbee" is in the Parish Records of Christ Church, Middlesex, Virginia. Phillis, a slave, bore a son named Gumbee on November 25. 1729. Phillis was a slave of Jacob Stiff. (National Society of the Colonial Dames of America in the Commonwealth of Virginia. Parish Register of Christ Church).

Likewise, Gumbys were found in plantation inventories and early census records in Virginia. A 1767 Westmoreland County, Virginia inventory of Captain Willoughby Newton's Home Plantation, shows a slave "Gumby" valued at fifty dollars. Newton recorded forty additional slaves as part of his property's inventory.

Ship manifest records noted slave owner James Gumby transporting slaves in December 1836 on the ship Barque Hortensia. The Hortensia sailed from the Port of Baltimore to Louisiana[3]. Louisiana slaves may have adapted the name of Gumby from this Gumby slave-owner or maintained their African Gombe/Gombeh names.

Abraham Stickley's "List of Free Negroes" in Shenandoah County, Virginia in 1843, contains the name Gumby. [4] Several researchers including Hill, [5] 1988, Chris Beneke, Christopher S. Grenda–2011, Joseph Brummell Earnest–1914. John B. Boles 1984, Douglas Chambers–2005 refer to an old African slave named "Dadda (Tom) Gumby." These references are found in texts addressing slave life, and religion in the Commonwealth of Virginia.

Nomini Hall was the home of Robert King Carter, the grandfather of Robert Carter III. Robert King Carter owned more than 1,000 slaves who lived on several plantation sites including

Nomini Hall, the home of Tom (Dadda) Gumby and his wife.

PHOTO 4. NOMINI HALL

Source: Wikipedia

Chapter 2
The Manumission

The Carter family of Virginia prospered from slave ownership. Thousands of slaves farmed crops on plantations throughout Virginia. The manumission written by Robert Carter III included several Gumby individuals. Carter announced his plan to free slaves on August 1, 1791, and completed the legal process by filing a Deed of Gift in Northumberland County, on September 5, 1791.[6] Among the slaves freed were; John Gumby and Nelson Gumby of Westmoreland and Frederick Counties, Virginia.[7] Robert Carter of Nomini Hall also freed Abby Gumby in Westmoreland County Virginia in January 1792[8]. The next year in 1793, Robert Carter freed another 30 slaves, eleven with the surname of Gumby. Following is one section of a transcript showing the freeing of slaves by Robert Carter[9]: "Abby Gumby, freed - *2 January 1792* Willoby Gumby, Sarah Gumby, Joan Gumby - freed *1 January 1793*."

The Gift of Deed entry for Nelson and Rachel Gumby, included the names of other Gumby families living on plantations in various counties. Although Carter's Deed of Gift enabled the manumitting of slaves, Carter retained Gumby family and others in slavery to allow them to learn trade skills.

Source: Deed of Gift

GUMBYS EMANCIPATED BY ROBERT CARTER III

> **Willoughby and Sarah Gumby**
> **January 1, 1793**
>
> > **Rose Gumby**
> > **January 1, 1797**
> >
> > **Tom Gumby**
> > **January 1, 1800**
> >
> > **Frances Gumby**
> > **January 1, 1802**
> >
> > **Humphrey Gumby**
> > **January 1, 1808**
> >
> > **Dorcas Gumby**
> > **January 1, 1809**

> **Nelson and Sarah J Gumby**
> **Nelson Jan. 1, 1794 - Sarah Jan. 1, 1798**
>
> > **Joan Gumby**
> > **January 1, 1803**
> >
> > **Dick Gumby**
> > **January 1, 1808**
> >
> > **James Gumby**
> > **January 1, 1811**
> >
> > **Nelson and Rachel's family lived on the Libra plantation**

Note: Nelson and Rachel Gumby gave birth to Nelson Gumby in 1791, Willoby in 1793, and Haney in 1795. (Barden)

Deed of Trust Emancipation

Robin and Sukey Gumby Robin - January 1, 1793 Sukey January 1, 1795	
Molly Gumby January 1, 1801	Dinah Gumby January 1, 1802
Jefse Gumby **January 1, 1803** / **Adam Gumby** **January 1, 1809**	**Family lived on Cancer Plantation**

When Robert Carter III decided to emancipate the slaves on his plantations, he exempted some of the slaves older than forty-five years of age. Robin Gumby was one of the exempt individuals. Robin was fifty-nine years old at the filing of the Deed of Emancipation.

Robert Carter's Deed identified the plantation, each person by their first name, age, the child's birth mother, the father, if applicable, and in some cases the spouse. Carter manumitted Abby Gumby of the Scorpio plantation January 2, 1792, and Joan Gumby age fifty-five of Old Ordinary plantation on January 1, 1793.

Photo 5 Robert Carter III
Source: Wikipedia Commons Photo

    Philip Vickers Fithian recorded the names of some slaves at Nomini Hall plantation in his diary.[10] The Nelson referenced by Fithian may have been Nelson Gumby. A section of Fithian's diary describes two waiting men Nelson, and Dennis. Nelson, age 14 in Carter's list, was a cabinetmaker in 1775, and in 1791 at the age of thirty-two Nelson worked as a joiner.[11]

Following manumission, John Gumby and Rachel Gumby are shown in the 1810 Census as free citizens of Fredrick County, Virginia.[12] ,Warren County also recorded Gumby families in later records as in the 1840 census.[13]

Plantations and County Locations

Robert "King" Carter had many slaves when he died in 1732. Carter's holdings included eighteen plantations:[14]

1. Nomini Hall - Westmoreland County
2. Corotoman–Lancaster County
3. Billingsgate–Richmond County
4. Old Ordinary–Westmoreland County
5. Forest Quarters–Westmoreland County
6. Mitchells Spread–Coles Point, Westmoreland County
7. Aquarius–Frederick County
8. Aries–Westmoreland County
9. Aries–Prince William County
10. Capricorn–Frederick County
11. Gemini–Westmoreland County
12. Leo (Oatlands)–Loudoun County
13. Libra–Frederick County
14. Pisces–the exact location of Pisces plantation is unknown
15. Sagittarius–Frederick County
16. Scorpio–Frederick County
17. Taurus–Westmoreland County
18. Virgo–Frederick County

Robert King Carter's holdings included 330,000 acres of land, and more than 1,000 slaves upon his death in 1732. Westmoreland and Frederick Counties held seventy-two percent (13 of 18) of his plantation holdings. Lancaster, Loudoun, Richmond, Prince William counties had one plantation each. The Pisces plantation county area is not documented.

Carter plantations

Carter writes of medical billings, and blankets for slaves, salt, and tallow. During Carter's time, animal fat was used to make "tallow" or soap. Tallow was used as balm for the skin. Carter may have cared about the health status of his slaves or he may have purchased balm to cover wounds caused by the abuse of slaves by overseers. (V. H. Society, Virginia Historical Society)

Carter's large plantations required skilled laborers. To accommodate plantation requirements, Carter trained his slaves in a wide-variety of jobs. A 1775 Census collected the names and occupations of residents in Westmoreland County. Carter identified the numbers of Nomini Hall Whites, slaves, and their work responsibilities. The slaves labored as millers, blacksmiths, colliers, shoemakers, wood carters, carpenters, cart men, coopers, postilions, and gardeners. (Whites and Blacks living at Nomony Hall in Westmoreland County, 1775)

Slaves also worked as laborers in the fields where tobacco, corn, wheat and other crops grew. Slave quarters were located near the main house. (Rockland, slave quarters, Leesburg, Loudoun County, Virginia) Dadda Gumby and his wife lived just 20 rods (110 yards, 100.5 meters), from Robert Carter III's plantation home as recorded in Philip Vickers Fithian's writings.

Chapter 3
Virginia Records

For over a century, slavery involved buying, selling, separating, and moving of Africans to plantations and farms. This separation caused families to lose their family histories. Slaves who didn't learn to read and write, utilized the oral tradition to pass on information about their families.

Through the years, the Gumby family history was spoken through the oral tradition. During these times, family members would record the history in writing, and share the information with other family members.

During the 1970s, Loretta Gumby Furman, and Janice Gumby Ramsey, recorded stories of the Gumby family history on visits to Mount Holly Springs, PA. Their grandparents, Harry Nelson Charles and Harriet Ann Gumby shared what they knew of the Gumby family. The family history sessions spoke of the lineage of John and Rachel Ellen Gumby, the father and mother of Harry Nelson Charles Gumby. Two of John's brothers, Samuel and Edward (Charles Edward) were referenced in the story-telling.

After the Nelson Gumby family migrated from Warren County, Virginia to Pennsylvania; legends about the move evolved. One family story is the crossing of the Pennsylvania State line by four brothers, John, Samuel, James, and Charles Edward. Another story is about Uncle Ed (Charles Edward) leaving Pennsylvania to live in another state. His brother, Sam was also said to be a traveler. Family members loved these stories and in telling them, the facts often changed.

PHOTO 6 GUMBY FAMILY HISTORY NOTES

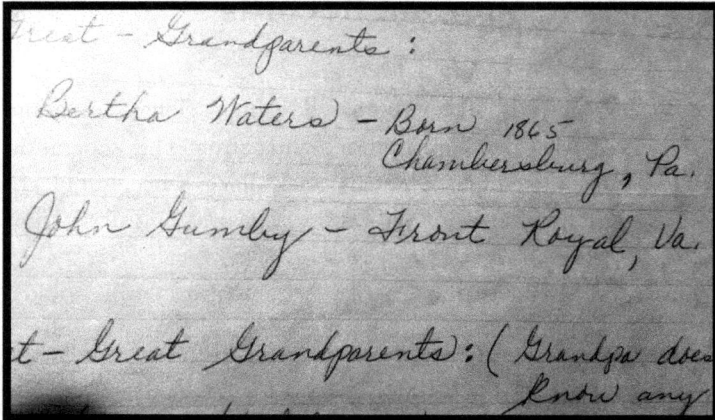

Front Royal Virginia became the focal point of the majority of stories expressed by family storytellers. Census records validate Front Royal, Warren County, Virginia as the home of several branches of the Gumbys. In addition, several Gumby families resided as free person in the Front Royal vicinity as early as 1840; several years prior to the onset of the Civil War. These facts provided information for further research.

In an interview, the author of this text recorded a note about a brother named "Jack." Reportedly Jack resided in Warren County at the same time as Nelson and Sarah Jane Gumby. The John Gumby shown in the 1800 Frederick County Tax list was referred as "Jack." Jack Gumby paid taxes in Frederick County between the years of 1822 and 1833. (MacDonald)

The Frederick County, Virginia Free Blacks Tax List

1800	John Gumby

• John Gumby owned one horse and paid $12 in tax during the years 1801-1802. John and his wife Diannah are on tax records in 1803,1804, 1805, 1810, and 1813 with one horse. John lists a son, 2 horses, and cattle.

1816	John Gumby and son Tom

• John and son Tom pay 1816 tax of $36 for 2 horses in 1816, and 1819. John Jr., appears on the tax list in 1835. In 1849 John pays taxes, and in 1850 John Gumby is assessed $1.00.

1814	Dick Gumby

• Dick Gumby pays tax on one horse in 1814. In 1817, Dick's tax is $18 for a horse, and taxes are paid from 1818, 1819, 1820. Old Dick Gumby is referenced during 1816 for a horse in the amount of $18.

1800	Nelson Gumby

• Nelson Gumby is on the 1800-1801 tax record. Nelson pays tax for one horse in 1802 through1803. Nelson is shown on the county tax from 1805-1861 when he is taxed for hogs and furniture.

1817	Tom Gumby

• Tom Gumby, the son of John Gumby is on the Frederick County tax list in 1817. From 1820-1831 he pays taxes for a horse beginning at $18 and $6 in 1831. Tom pays taxes through 1835.

1814	Elijah Gumby

• Elijah is on the 1835 tax list in various years through 1860. In 1850, one male and 1 free individual are noted, as well as two males in 1853.

Source: (MacDonald)

Tax List Comments

✓ Gumby family members established themselves in their fields of work immediately after manumission. The 1800 – 1859 tax lists show the acquisition of property by former slaves and their offspring. Tax lists revealed the names of spouses and in some cases included the names of their children.

✓ John Gumby and Nelson Gumby are the two earliest Gumbys to appear in the 1800 Frederick County tax list. Willoughby Gumby appeared in the 1800 Westmoreland County Tax List. The Frederick County 1803 entry names Dinah as John Gumby's wife. John Gumby's son Tom appears in 1815, and John Gumby Jr. in 1835.

✓ Nelson Gumby appears on the Frederick County Tax list in 1800. Nelson and his wife Rachel are shown on the 1803 tax record. Nelson and Rachel Gumby's son, Richard is shown living with his mother Rachel on the 1813 Frederick County tax list. Dick (Richard) was three years old in 1791, during the writing of the Gift of Deed. In 1813, Dick would have been a young man of twenty-five. Nelson Gumby and his family are found living in Warren County, Virginia as early as 1852. The 1860 Frederick County tax records show Nelson paying taxes through 1861. Likewise, Nelson's family is shown residing in Frederick County and Warren County during the 1860 Census.

✓ Elijah Gumby appears on the Frederick County Tax Lists in 1835. Census show Elijah's birth as 1810 on the 1860 Frederick County, Virginia Census. The 1850 tax list shows one male boy, and one free. Elijah's tax is one dollar for that year.

- ✓ In 1853 Elijah is taxed for two males, four hogs, (four dollars), and furniture (fifteen dollars). Seven years following the tax year of 1853, the 1860 Census shows Robert age sixteen, and a twelve-year old Elijah Gumby working at the home of the Robinson family in Magisterial District 5, Frederick County. If these two individuals were in the household of Elijah in 1853, Robert would have been nine years old and Elijah five years old.

- ✓ The Frederick County Tax Lists indicated the former slaves of Robert Carter III as Carter's "Free Negroes," as shown next to the names of John Gumby and Nelson Gumby. Since John Gumby (also known as Jack) and Nelson Gumby are listed together on the 1800 Census and the Frederick County Tax List, the pair may have been brothers. When examining page ten of Carter's Deed of Emancipation, Nelson, age twenty-four lives at Libra with his wife Rachel. John, age twenty-three also lives at Libra with his wife Dinah, age seventeen, and their daughter, two-year old Liddia.

- ✓ John Gumby, (or John Jr.) hired himself out in 1851 for work to satisfy unpaid taxes. [15]

African Migration to Front Royal, Virginia

Warren County, Virginia became home to many free Negroes. Robert Carter held land north of Front Royal, VA. Farris contends Robert Carter III and other slave owners held thousands of slaves in Warren and Clarke counties and throughout the Shenandoah Valley. (Farris). According to Farris, there were more than one hundred Blacks living in the Freetown and Southtown communities of Front Royal.

Gumbys living in 1850 Front Royal, Virginia (69th district,) were Thomas and Hannah Gumby, and their children James, Sarah,

Nancy, and Cordelia. Other Gumbys residing in the Sixty-Ninth District of Warren County were Mary Gumby, and Letty Gumby.

FIGURE 1. 1850 WARREN COUNTY GUMBY CENSUS, VIRGINIA

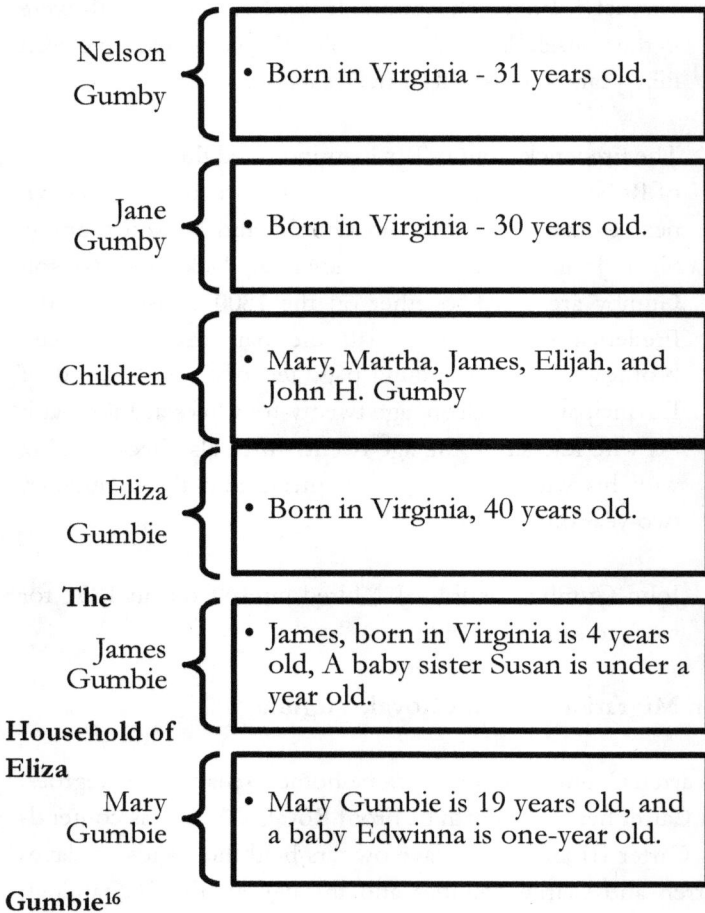

Nelson Gumby	• Born in Virginia - 31 years old.
Jane Gumby	• Born in Virginia - 30 years old.
Children	• Mary, Martha, James, Elijah, and John H. Gumby
Eliza Gumbie	• Born in Virginia, 40 years old.
The James Gumbie	• James, born in Virginia is 4 years old, A baby sister Susan is under a year old.
Household of Eliza Mary Gumbie	• Mary Gumbie is 19 years old, and a baby Edwinna is one-year old.

Gumbie[16]

United States 1840 Census, Database with images (2016)

DOCUMENT 1. NELSON GUMBY AS A FREE MAN

Nelson and Thomas Gumby appear on the "List of Free Negroes in Warren County in 1855.

Source: Library of Virginia

Thomas Gumby, the son of John and Dianah Richards Gumby moved from Frederick County to Warren County, Virginia. Thomas and his wife Hannah, James, age nineteen, Sarah who was seventeen, four-year old Nancy, and two-year old Cordelia lived in the household.

Although Thomas Gumby and his family moved to Warren County, records show Tom owed One-dollar in tax to Frederick County Virginia in 1859.

A family headed by fifty-four-year-old Henrietta Gumby is found in the Census records. In 1850 twenty-nine-year-old W.S. Eliza Gumby, seventeen-year-old Barbara Gumby, ten-year old James Gumby, four-year old Henrietta Gumby, four-year old William S. Gumby, and one-year old Sarah L. Gumby are identified in Henrietta's household.

Nelson Gumby and his family moved to Warren County Virginia by 1850. Nelson's free registration is recorded in the 1852 Warren County Court. Census records show Frederick County included Nelson and his family in the 1860 Census.

Below is information recorded in the Frederick County 1860 Census.

1. Nelson Gumby, Male, 41 years, born in Virginia

2. Sarah J. Gumby, Female, 40 years, born in Virginia

3. Mary E. Gumby, Female, 17 years, born in Virginia

4. James W. Gumby, Male, 15 years, born in Virginia

5. Elijah Gumby, Male, 14 years, born in Virginia

6. John H. Gumby, Male, 12 years, born in Virginia

7. Evaline Gumby, Female, 10 years, born in Virginia

8. Samuel Gumby, Male, 9 years, born in Virginia

9. Jacob Gumby, Male, 7 years, born in Virginia

10. Eli Gumby, Male 2 years, born in Virginia

11. Sarah Gumby, 1 year, born in Virginia

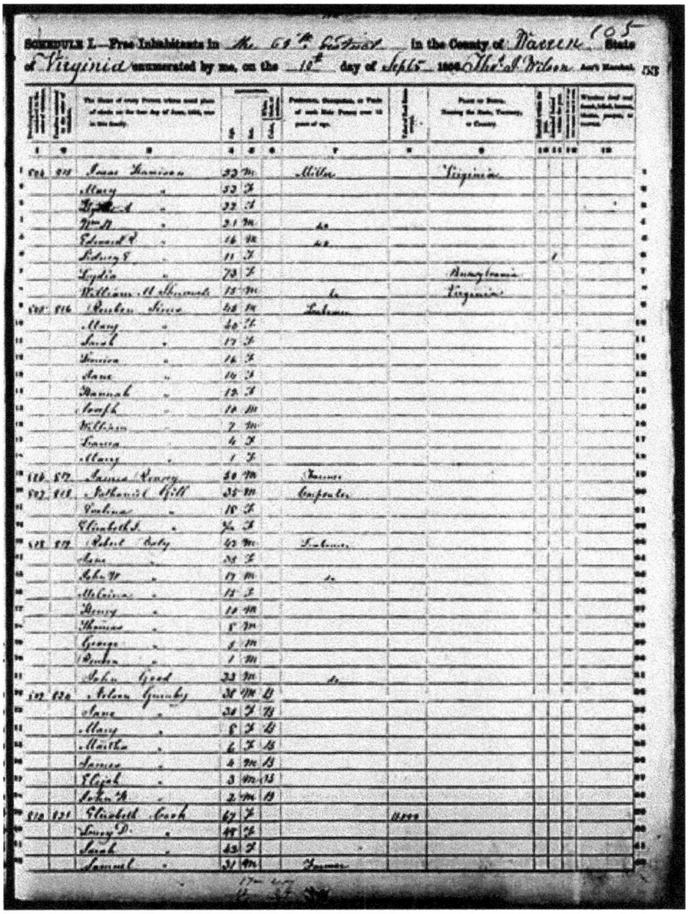
SCHEDULE I.—Free Inhabitants in the 6th District in the County of Warren State of Virginia enumerated by me, on the 10th day of Sept 1860.

DOCUMENT 2. 1860 WARREN, VIRGINIA CENSUS

Chapter 4
Mount Holly Springs, PA

Following the Civil War, Gumby surnamed individuals migrated from Virginia toward the North, and Eastern states of Maryland, Delaware and Pennsylvania. Members of the Nelson and Jane Gumby family of Virginia, migrated to Pennsylvania, to the towns of Barnitz, and Newville in Cumberland County. The new residents found work as laborers, factory, and mill workers.

Gumby families moved to the Borough of Mount Holly Springs after living in Barnitz. Beginning in 1869, freed slaves settled at the base of a mountain range, and named the area Mount Tabor. The settlement contained a school, a church and a cemetery. The church was named the Mount Tabor African Methodist Episcopal Zion Church. The cemetery was named Mount Tabor, however, the citizens of Mount Holly Springs referred to the burial ground as the Mount Holly Colored Cemetery.

Along with other freed slaves, the Mount Tabor area created its own community. The 1870 Census contains a record for the Nelson Gumby family living in Cumberland County, Pennsylvania.

DOCUMENT 3, 1870 CUMBERLAND COUNTY CENSUS

Nelson Gumby
- Age 52
- Born in Virginia

Jane Gumby
- Age 48
- Born in Virginia

Catherine Gumby
- Age 13
- Born in Virginia

Source – Familysearch.org US 1870 Census Records

The Nelson Gumby family is settled in the town of Barnitz, Pennsylvania by 1880. The area was referred to as Newville. Jane S. Gumby, age fifty, is living with her thirty-two-year-old daughter Elisabeth, sons James, and John H. N. Gumby, Charles E. Gumby, and grandchildren; twelve-year-old John Gumby, ten-year-old Sarah J. Gumby, and one-year-old Julian.

The Parsonage

Picture Courtesy of the H. N. Gumby F amily Archives

PHOTO 7. THE MOUNT TABOR AMEZ CHURCH PARSONAGE

The Gumby Escape to Freedom[17]
by Donald E. Owens of Carlisle, PA

The Gumby's were slaves until emancipation by their slave owner Robert Carter III. Although segments of the Gumby family were freed slaves, the majority of Blacks in the United States were not freed until after the Civil War. The following story was passed along through the family descendants of Nelson Gumby and shared by Donald Owens, the son of Sarah Elizabeth Gumby.

"Samuel Gumby and one of his brothers, (name unknown) out-raced a group of slave catchers to cross the Virginia state line to Pennsylvania. Although the family of Samuel were free inhabitants of Virginia, other Blacks were enslaved. Samuel and a brother decided they wanted to travel to Pennsylvania. Free inhabitants living in Virginia told the brothers if they were to travel, to run and hide until they were far enough into Pennsylvania for safety reasons."

When Sam and his brother left Virginia one day, slave catchers were right behind them on horses chasing them as fast as the horses could run. Once Sam and his brother crossed the Mason-Dixon Line, they stopped to hide behind some trees. The slave catchers stopped the chase and stared at Sam and his brother. At a certain point in Pennsylvania, slave catchers could not cross into the free lands of the State. The slave catchers turned around and headed south back into slave territory.

Reportedly, Samuel and his brother were told to travel to Barnitz Mill, Pennsylvania where they could find lodging, food, and a job. Later other Gumby's from Virginia joined them at Barnitz Mill where the families settled prior to moving to Mount Holly Springs, Pennsylvania.

Donald Owens tells the entire story of the Gumby family's migration to Barnitz Pennsylvania through an interview with the Cumberland County Historical Society. The interview is available from the Elizabeth V. and George F. Gardner Digital Library; http://gardnerlibrary.org/stories/donald-e-owens-sr (Donald E. Owens).

John H. Gumby's Baptism Record

DOCUMENT 4 ENTRY OF JOHN GUMBY'S BAPTISM

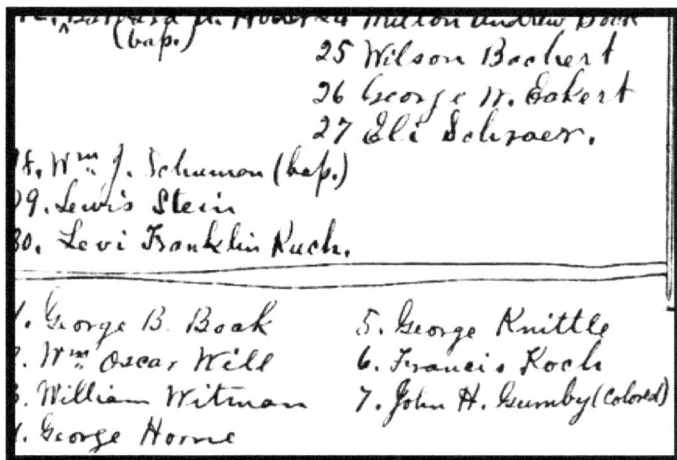

Source: Familysearch.org

The Baptism record of John H. Gumby shows the date of May 10, 1879. The baptism occurred at the St. Paul's Evangelical Lutheran Church in Orwigsburg, Township, and Schuylkill, Pennsylvania. John Gumby, labeled as number seven, was the only African American baptized within the group and is noted as "colored" on the church record.

In 1880, John H Gumby possibly lived and worked in Orwigsburg, Township, and Schuylkill, Pennsylvania. John was twenty-eight years old. The evidence of working in the area may support the record of John H. Gumby's baptism at the St. Paul's church in 1879.[18] It is not known if John became an active member of this church.

Education

Among the five schools in Cumberland County in the late 19th century, one school was African American.[19] The school was noted as colored according to a historical review of the Borough. Although a photograph of the actual school was not located for this book. The picture below is an example of an African-American school building following slavery. This structure is located in Vienna, Virginia.

Photograph: Library of Congress
PHOTO 8 A VIRGINIA SLAVE CABIN

The Mount Tabor Community

The African American community of Mount Holly Springs, PA was called "Mount Tabor" by its residents. Most of the first residents of this community were freed slaves from Virginia. In 1900, there were over 100 African Americans in the area. (R. G. Bauchum) The name of Mount Tabor was never officially adopted by the town of Mt. Holly Springs, and the area was referred to as "colored" or "smoky row."

African American families living in Mount Holly Springs included the following names; Calloway, Jordon, Hopwell, Gumby, Holland, Townsend, Johnson, Burd, Parker, Bowman, Foe, Howard, Furman, Moore, Watson, McFarland, Whiten, Brown, Tyson, Wilkerson, Jones, Ward, and Tarleton.

Most families consisting of former slaves and their descendants from Clarke, Frederick, Warren, Westmoreland, Loudoun, and Richmond Counties in Virginia.

African American families worshipped at the Mount Tabor African Methodist Episcopal Zion Church. The church was a vibrant worship and community gathering place after the Civil War through the 1970s. Through the years, the church was pastored by Rev. Anderson, Rev. Bullock, Rev. Nichols, Rev. Hightower, Rev. Thomas, Rev. Kenneth Wallace and Rev. Lena Parr.

Stories of enslavement are told in Civil War depositions of Lucinda Johnson Parker, wife of Elias V. Parker born a slave in 1827 in Clarke County, VA. (R. Bauchum). Henry Johnson, Lucinda's father was born a slave in Virginia in 1830. Henry's wife Jane E. Johnson was born in 1835. Judith Bowman, a former slave and a resident of the Mount Holly African American community tells of being enslaved in Virginia with Elias Parker and other residents of Mount Tabor.

Many of the homes in the Mt. Tabor area were log homes as described by Harry Lester Gumby. Ethel Gumby described several "shanty-style" homes along Mountain (Smoky) Road. These shanties were occupied by African American families.

The Church was constructed from logs and planks. The church structure is in the process of rehabilitation by local historical and preservation groups.

PHOTO 9 **MOUNT TABOR AFRICAN METHODIST EPISCOPAL ZION CHURCH**

Photo courtesy of the Harry Nelson Gumby Family

The Gumby House in Mount Holly Springs

The home in the photograph witnessed eight generations of the Johnson, Parker, and Gumby families. Through the years, the address of this home included; 136 Mounted Route, 136 Mountain Road, and 70 Mountain Street.

Photograph. courtesy of the Harry N. Gumby Family
.

PHOTO 10. WEST STREET AME ZION CHURCH
Google Image © 2015

African Americans have worshiped at the West Street African Methodist Episcopal Zion Church for over one hundred and twenty years. [20] The Gumby family served as members of this congregation, and continue to worship at West Street Church in Mount Holly Springs, Pennsylvania.

Chapter 5
The Military

The Civil War - On October 3, 1863, the War Department issued General Order 329 as a means to facilitate recruitment into the United States Colored Troops. General Order 329 contained a section that allowed local slave owners in Union controlled territories to permit and even demand their slaves enlist in the military service. Slave owners were compensated for authorizing their respective slave to enlist in the Union Army. The average amount of compensation to each owner was three hundred dollars.

Several Gumby men served as soldiers in the United States Colored Troops during the Civil War. Jeremiah Gumby of Delaware,[21] and John Gumby enlisted with the Tennessee Infantry. Other Civil War USCT soldiers with the Gumby surname included men from Virginia, Maryland, Delaware, New York, Washington DC, Louisiana, and Pennsylvania. Soldiers joining the United States Colored Troops included the following men;

1. Amos Gumby, 82nd Regiment, United States Colored Infantry, Louisiana, Gulf Coast.
2. Anthony Gumby, 151st Regiment, New York Infantry, New York.
3. Jacob Gumby, 81st Regiment, United States Colored Infantry, Louisiana Gulf Coast.
4. Jeremiah Gumby, 22nd Regiment, Company D, United States Colored Infantry, Virginia. (Jeremiah Gumby survived the War).
5. Jeremiah Gumby, 25th Regiment, United States Colored Infantry Pennsylvania.
6. John Gumby, 7th Regiment, United States Colored Troops, Maryland. (John Gumby survived the War).
7. Lewis Gumby, 81st Regiment, United States Colored Infantry, Louisiana Gulf Coast.
8. Noah Gumby, 28th Regiment, United States Colored Troops, Indiana.
9. Noel Gumby, 82nd Regiment, United States Colored Infantry, Louisiana, Gulf Coast.
10. William Gumby, 7th Regiment, Company D, United States Colored Infantry, Maryland.
11. William Gumby, 22nd Regiment, United States Colored Infantry, Virginia. (William Gumby survived the War).
12. William Gumby, 25th Regiment, United States Colored Infantry, Pennsylvania. (William Gumby survived the War).
13. William Gumby, 1st Regiment District of Columbia Calvary, Washington DC (William Gumby survived the War).

Some soldiers chose their respective surnames. Military records of two of the USCT soldiers with the surname of Gumby were shown as "alias."

Shown is the flag of the Pennsylvania Second Infantry, United States Colored Troops.

Library of Congress

The image shown is a military record of William Gumby, 7th Regiment, Company D, United States Colored Infantry, Maryland. (N. A. Administration)

DOCUMENT 5. WILLIAM GUMBY USCT

Military Records of Noah Gumby
Source: National Archives and Records Administration

DOCUMENT 6. NOAH GUMBY ENLISTMENT

Source National Archives and Records Administration Fold 3

World War I

Harry Nelson Charles Gumby registered for the draft during World War I. At the onset of the war, many African American men registered after a law mandated the registration of men over the age of twenty-one. Although Harry Nelson Charles Gumby didn't enter the Army, most family members were unaware that he had registered to serve in the military during World War I.

National Archives and Records Administration, Fold 3

William Henry Gumby's World War I Registration

Source: National Archives and Records Administration

DOCUMENT 7. WILLIAM H. GUMBY DRAFT CARD

Draft Registration Card

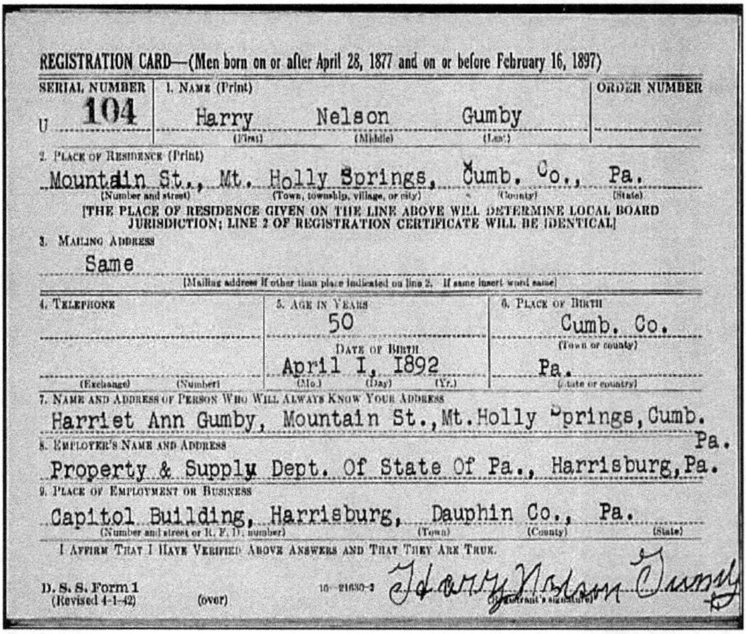

World War II Registration of Harry Nelson Charles Gumby

In 1942, Harry Nelson Charles Gumby registered for World War II at the age of fifty. This image is a copy of his draft registration card. Despite Harry Nelson Gumby's age, all persons born between the years of 1877 and 1897 were required to register for military service.

PHOTO 11 HARRY GUMBY REGISTRATION
Source – Familysearch.org

DOCUMENT 8. WAR CARD OF GEORGE W. GUMBY

Source: (N. A. Administration)

Harry Lester Gumby was the only son of Harry Nelson Charles Gumby to serve an entire career in the armed forces. Harry served twenty-eight years in the military. Harry was stationed at Camp Crowder, Nevada Missouri; Dyess Air Force Base Abilene, Texas; Brooks Field, San Antonio Texas; Lockbourne Army Airfield, Columbus Ohio; Fort Dix Army Post, Fort Dix, New Jersey; Goose Bay Air Force Base, Labrador (Greenland); Hickam Air Force Base, Honolulu Hawaii; and Richards-Gebaur Air Force Base, Grandview, Missouri. Harry served special duty assignments in Japan, the Philippine Islands and Guam.

Gumby Family in the Armed Forces

The descendants of Nelson Gumby have served with honor in the United States military as outlined;

Air Force

- Charles Edward Gumby
- Charles R. Washington
- Harry L. Gumby
- Janelle Henderson
- Ronald E. Gumby Jr.
- William H. Gumby Jr.
- William Lester Gumby
- Carl Lathaire Owens
- James Trigg II

Army

- Edgar Leroy Gumby
- John Cameron Gumby
- John Wesley Gumby
- Robert W. Gumby
- Robert Owens

Marine Corps

- Charles Edward Gumby
- Ronald E. Gumby

Navy

- Charles Henderson Jr.

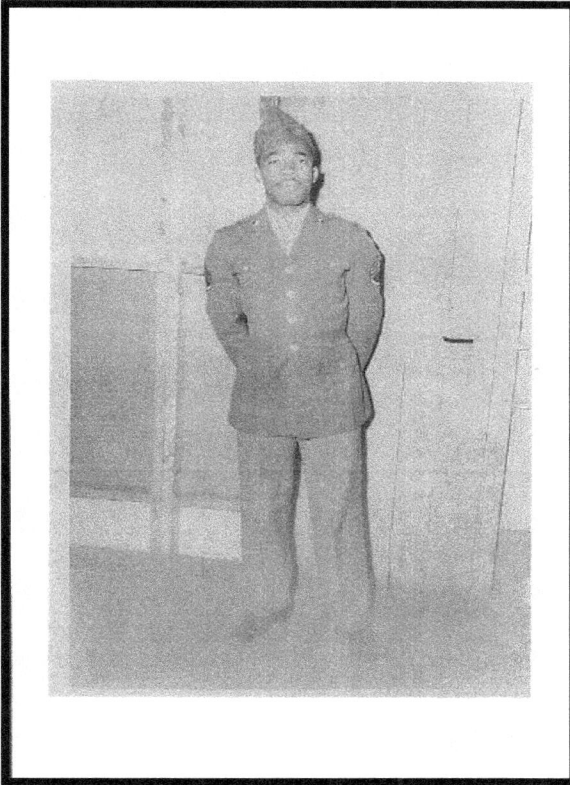

Photo: Courtesy of Ethel, Edna, and Harriet Gumby

Chief Master Sargent Harry L. Gumby received a posthumous award from President Barack Obama in 2014. CMSgt Harry Lester Gumby died July 31, 2014.

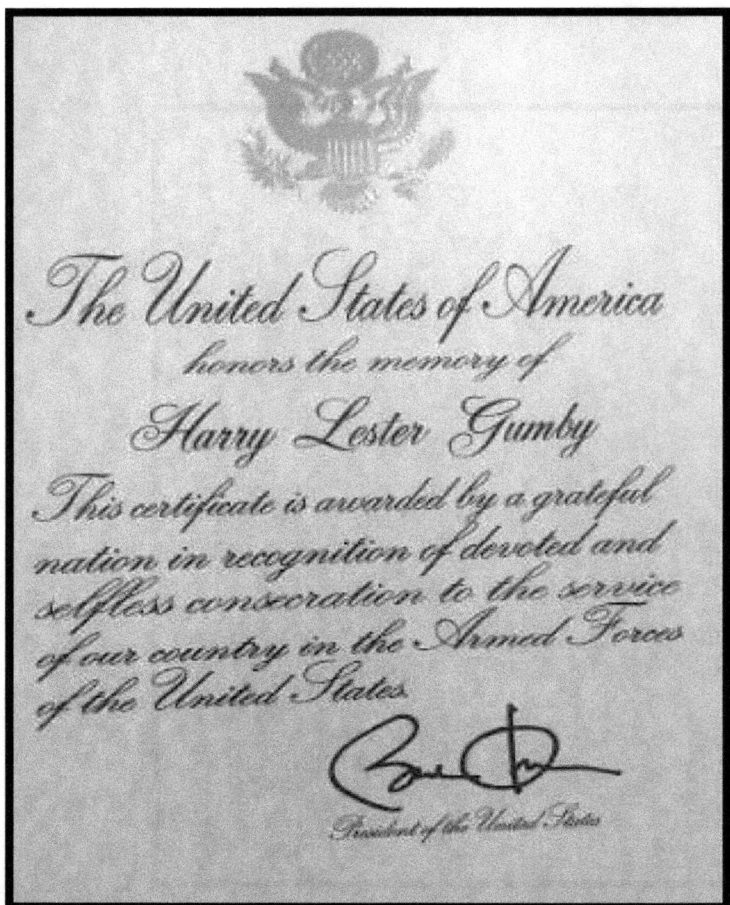

DOCUMENT 9. PRESIDENTIAL SERVICE AWARD

Part II
The Gumby Descendants

Chapter 6
Professional Careers

Business and Professional Careers

During the 1800s, slaves labored in the plantation fields. Although slaves worked in the fields, Robert Carter III trained his slaves as artisans, carpenters, cabinetmakers and in other trades. These slaves built houses, cabins, tools, furniture, wagons, and other items.

In 1792, Gumby slaves began emancipation. Free citizens of Virginia had to maintain jobs, or leave the state. The earliest records of free African Americans show occupations as carpenters, milliners, laborers, cooks, farmers, and drivers.

Free Black men worked as tailors, culinary workers, musicians, and transporters of wood, supplies, and food. The 1900 Census of Mount Holly Springs, PA shows African Americans working as teamsters, hotel cooks, barbers, mill, and factory workers, and ammunition makers.

Henry W. Spradley; A Respected Professional

Henry W. Spradley worked in the position of janitor at Dickinson College in Carlisle PA. Born a slave June 6, 1830; Henry moved to Pennsylvania from Frederick County, Virginia. He served in the United States Colored Troops, 24th Regiment, Company G, and began working at the college in 1879.

When Henry Spradley died, an article was featured in an edition of the "Dickinson" newspaper on April 17, 1897. (Sigmund). (Henry was not a relative of the Gumby family.)

Esther Popel Shaw was the first African American Woman to graduate Dickinson College in 1919. As a student, Esther was not allowed to live in the dormitory for women. (Bitts-Jackson) William Lynn Gumby, son of Harry Nelson Charles and Harriet Parker Gumby, received a degree in the sciences from Dickenson College in 1954.

PHOTO 12 HENRY SPRADLEY

LIBRARY OF CONGRESS

Gumby Family Professions and Business

Gumby descendants serve in diverse professions throughout the United States. Timothy and Stephenae Gumby are the owners of Gumby's Barber Shop, 3841 Main Street in Kansas City, MO. Timothy is the son of Harry Bernard Gumby III, and the grandson of Harry Lester (Doris) Gumby.

Harry Charles Nelson (Harriet) Gumby are Timothy's great-grandparents; John H. (Rachel) Gumby are his second great-grand parents; and Timothy is the third great-grandson of Nelson (Sarah Jane) Gumby. Timothy is the fourth great-grandson of Nelson Gumby, born in 1791. Nelson and Rachel Gumby emancipated by Robert Carter III are Timothy's fifth-great-grandparents.

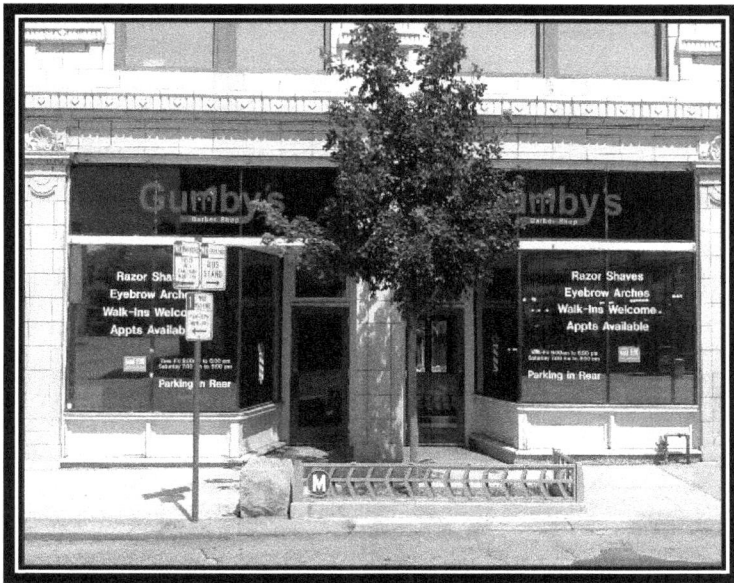

PHOTO 13. GUMBY'S BARBERSHOP
Source: Photograph courtesy of Gumby's Barbershop

The Gumby individuals presented in this section are the descendants of Nelson and Rachel Gumby, freed by the Deed of Emancipation of 1791. This section highlights, and honors the professions of family members.[22] Each section lists the name and the category description.

Business

- Brian E. and Michelle Gines, Owners of Purpose Publishing Company, and Millennium Catering Company. Grandview, Missouri.

PHOTO 14. PURPOSE PUBLISHING COMPANY

IMAGE COURTESY OF BRIAN AND MICHELLE GINES

- Jessica A. Bauchum, Co-Owner, Bauchum Sisters Music Business & Performing Arts, Dallas Texas.

- Stephanie L. Bauchum, Owner, Bye Fat; Hello Fit, Health Blog and Apparel, Owner; Nanny Tees, Co-owner, Bauchum Sisters Music Business & Performing Arts, Dallas Texas.
- Timothy Erin Gumby, Business Owner, Gumby's Barber Shop, Kansas City, Missouri.

Education

- Anna Elizabeth Gumby Krishnappa, PhD. Retired. The School District of Philadelphia.
- Bobby Eugene Gines, PhD, Retired Assistant Superintendent, Riverview Garden School District, St. Louis, Missouri.
- Brenda Gumby Gines MS, PhD, Retired Educator, Riverview Gardens School District, St. Louis Missouri, and the Kansas City Missouri School District.
- Edgar L. Gumby, dec'd, Educator, Neptune Township School District, Neptune, New Jersey.
- Jacqueline Todd Sweeney, Retired Educator, Neptune Township School District, Neptune, New Jersey.
- Janice Gumby (Sweeney) Ramsey MS, Retired Principal, Neptune Township School District, Neptune, New Jersey.
- Jason E. Gines, PhD, Professor, and Director of the Office of Multicultural Affairs, College of Information Sciences and Technology, Pennsylvania State University, State College, Pennsylvania.
- Jessica A. Bauchum, MS. Educator, Plano Independent School District, Plano, Texas, Pepin Academies, Riverview, Florida.
- John Wesley Gumby, PhD, Retired Superintendent, School Administrator, The School District of Philadelphia; Harrisburg School District; Professor, Pennsylvania State University, Middletown.
- Kathryn J. Gines, PhD, Professor and Founding Director, Collegium of Black Women Philosophers, Pennsylvania State University, State College, Pennsylvania.

- Loretta Gumby Furman dec'd, Education, Neptune Township School District, Neptune, New Jersey.
- Millicent R. Gines Connor MS, Educator, Grandview Consolidated School District # 4, Grandview, Missouri.

Faith-Based Ministry

- Elder John Wesley Gumby, PhD, United House of Prayer for All People, Harrisburg, PA
- Elder Linda Baltimore Green Gumby, Th.D. United Holy Church of America. Founder and Chief Executive Officer, Emanuel's Cornerstone Ministry, Harrisburg, PA
- Elder Robert W. Gumby, Lingo Memorial Church of God in Christ, Inc. Harrisburg PA
- Minister Brian Eugene Gines, New Life in Christ International Ministries, Grandview, MO.
- Minister Jessica Bauchum, Friendship West Baptist Church, Dallas, TX.
- Rev. Ada Sanders Richardson, Bible Tabernacle Christian Center, York, PA.

Federal and State Service

- Charles R. Washington, dec'd. Pennsylvania Department of Transportation.
- Edna C. Gumby, Retired, Federal Civil Service, Harrisburg, Pennsylvania.
- Harry C. Nelson Gumby dec'd, Pennsylvania State Department of Property and Supplies.
- John C. Gumby dec'd, Federal Civil Service, Harrisburg, Pennsylvania.
- Kimberly Johnson (Gumby) Payne, Department of Homeland Security, Kansas City, Missouri.
- Dr. Linda M. Baltimore Gumby Green, American Federation of State, County and Municipal Employees, Harrisburg Pennsylvania.
- Lori J. Stanton Harris, United States Department of the Army, Huntsville, Alabama.

- Mary Evelyn Gumby dec'd, Federal Civil Service, Harrisburg, Pennsylvania.
- Michael L. Gumby, Federal Civil Service, Harrisburg, Pennsylvania.
- Pauline E. Gumby Sanders dec'd, Pennsylvania Department of Transportation.
- Raymond Lloyd Gumby dec'd, LetterKenny Army Depot, Chambersburg, Pennsylvania.
- Rosalind Gumby Bauchum, Federal Civil Service, United States Census Bureau, Kansas City, Missouri.
- Stephen D. Gumby, Department of Homeland Security, Lee's Summit, MO.
- Angela Gumby, Commonwealth of Pennsylvania, Department of Human Services.

Law Enforcement

- Ashley Furman, Security and Corrections, Neptune, New Jersey.
- Charles R. Washington, dec'd. District of Columbia Police Department.
- Darrell Edward Gumby, dec'd, Pennsylvania State Police.
- Darrell Jay Furman, Retired Detective, Neptune Police Department, Neptune, New Jersey.
- Derrick Williams, Mississippi State Police, Jackson MS
- Harry Bernard Gumby III, Retired, Kansas City Police Department, Reserve Squad, Kansas City, Missouri.
- Raymond Lloyd Gumby, dec'd, Shippensburg Auxiliary Police, Cumberland County Fire Police Association, Fraternal Order of Police Lodge 94, Shippensburg, Pennsylvania.
- Richard Lester Gumby, Pennsylvania State Police.
- Ronald E. Gumby Sr., Federal Police, United States Department of Defense.

Military Service

- Charles Edward Gumby, United States Marines.
- Charles R. Washington, dec'd. United States Air Force.

- Earl Warren Arter, United States Air Force.
- Edgar L. Gumby, dec'd, United States Army.
- Harry Lester Gumby, dec'd, United States Army Air Corps, United States Air Force.
- James Trigg, United States Air Force.
- John C. Gumby, dec'd, United States Army.
- John Wesley Gumby, United States Army.
- Julius D. Ramsey, United States Army, Retired.
- Robert W. Gumby, United States Army.
- Robert L. Owens, dec'd, United States Army.
- Ronald E. Gumby, United States Marines.
- William H. Gumby, Jr., United States Air Force.
- William Lester Gumby, dec'd. United States Air Force.

Professional

- Alicia Stanton Thames, Retail and Business Services, Neptune New Jersey.
- Arvetta Gumby, Insurance Auditing, Real Estate, Kansas City, Missouri.
- Derrick Williams, Commercial Insurance, Overland Park, Kansas.
- Donald Owens, dec'd, Manufacturing and Business, Pennsylvania.
- Ethel L. Gumby, Retired, Business, Mt. Holly Springs, Pennsylvania.
- Harriet L. Gumby, Retired, Telecommunications, Bell Laboratories, New Jersey.
- Harry L. Gumby, dec'd, Health Care Administrator, Kansas City, Missouri.
- James William A. Bauchum, Business and Contracting, Kansas and Missouri.
- Jennifer Sweeney, Business Affairs, New Jersey.
- John C. Gumby, dec'd, Transportation, New Cumberland, Pennsylvania.
- Juliet Clark Gumby, Retired, Allied Health and Medical Care Services, Kansas City, Missouri.

- Lisa C. Gumby Williams, Insurance, Account Executive, Kansas City, Missouri.
- Lucinda Jane Gumby, dec'd, Personal Services, Carlisle, Pennsylvania.
- Marqus A. A. Bibbs, Graphic Designer, Kansas City, Missouri.
- ,Quint K. Connor, Business and Technology, Overland Park, Kansas.
- Rosalind Gumby Bauchum, Health and Human Services. Owner and Managing Principal, R. G. Bauchum & Associates, Inc., Researcher and Author. Grandview, Missouri.
- Stephenae Williams Gumby, Mutual Fund Investments, Kansas City, Missouri.
- Thomas David Gumby, Vocal Arts, and Community and Neighborhood Services, Carlisle, Pennsylvania.
- Tracy Gumby, Telecommunications, Technology and Business, Carlisle, Pennsylvania.
- William L. Gumby, Retired Chemist, Retired Rochester New York.

Civic, Community, and Panhellenic Involvement

- Ada Pauline Sanders Richardson, Delta Sigma Theta Sorority, Incorporated.
- Angela Denise Gumby, Delta Sigma Theta Sorority, Incorporated.
- Arvetta K. Gumby Prewitt, Alpha Kappa Alpha Sorority, Incorporated, The National Association of Negro Business and Professional Women's Club Inc., Metropolitan Kansas City Club. and The Sisterhood.
- Brenda Gumby Gines, National Education Association, National Association of Negro Business and Professional Women's Clubs, Inc., National Association of Christian Counselors.
- Charles R. Washington, dec'd. Fraternal Order of Metropolitan Washington Police, Haines-Stackfield American Legion Post 826.
- Debra K. Sanders, Alpha Kappa Alpha Sorority, Inc.

- Ethel L. Gumby, Deborah Grand Chapter Order of Eastern Star, Prince Hall Adopted of Commonwealth of Pennsylvania, 50-year Member.
- Harry Bernard Gumby III, National Christian Bikers Association, National Black Bikers Association. Founder of God's Wheels, Inc.
- Jacqueline Todd Sweeney, National Education Association.
- Janice Gumby Ramsey, Alpha Kappa Alpha Sorority, Incorporated, New Jersey International Educators, Monmouth County Elementary Principals Association, National Education Association, National Association of Negro Business and Professional Women's Club, Inc., Institute for Educational Leadership, Monmouth County Human Relations Commission.
- Jessica Ann Bauchum, Sigma Alpha Iota, Professional Music Fraternity for Women Inc., and the Association of Professional Texas Educators, Inc.
- John Cameron Gumby, dec'd, Letort Star Lodge 18, 33rd degree in Unit 9, member, Past Master and Secretary of Most Worshipful Prince Hall Grand Lodge Jeptha Chapter 4, Order of Eastern Star, serving as Past Worthy Patron, Himyar Templar 17, Nimrod Consistory 9, and American Legion Post 826 of Carlisle, Pa.
- John Wesley Gumby, Omega Phi Psi Fraternity Incorporated, Prince Hall Masons, Chosen Friends Lodge No. 43, F. & A.M.
- Lori Jo Stanton Harris, Delta Sigma Theta Sorority, Incorporated.
- Millicent Gines Connor, Inc., Alpha Kappa Alpha Sorority, Inc., National Education Association.
- Naomi Ruth (Banks) Ross, dec'd. Eastern Star P.H.A. 5th District Jeptha #4.
- Pauline E. Gumby Sanders dec'd, Republican Committee Woman and Community Activist.

- Rosalind A. Gumby Bauchum, Alpha Kappa Alpha Sorority, Incorporated, Greater Kansas City, and the Metropolitan Kansas City Clubs of the National Association of Negro Business and Professional Women's Clubs, Inc., Midwest Afro-American Genealogy Interest Coalition, Association for the Study of African American Life and History, Kansas City Study Group, Northern Neck Virginia Historical Society.

- Earl Warren Arter, Haines-Stackfield American Legion Post 826.

PHOTO 15. EDGAR GUMBY SINGS
WITH CHOIR

Edgar Gumby is shown with a young adult choir. The name of the choir is unknown. Edgar is on the last row, fifth person from the right.

Courtesy of Ethel, Edna, Harriet, and William Gumby Family

Educational Institutions

Edgar L. Gumby, John Wesley Gumby, and Anna E. Gumby Krishnappa attended the historic Cheney State Teachers College (now Cheyney University of Pennsylvania). Founded in 1837, Cheney University is the oldest institutional college for African Americans in the United States. John Wesley Gumby was the first Cheyney student to graduate with a major in French, Spanish, and Linguistics in 1968.

Gumby family members attended the following institutions of higher education;

o   Avila University of Missouri
o   Bloomsburg University of Pennsylvania
o   Caldwell College of New Jersey
o   The University of Central Missouri
o   Central Penn College
o   Cheyney University of Pennsylvania
o   Columbia State University, Louisiana
o   Delaware State University
o   Dickinson College of Pennsylvania
o   Elizabethtown College, Pennsylvania
o   Elohim Bible College and School of Counseling
o   East Stroudsburg University, Pennsylvania
o   Emory University of Georgia
o   Grand Canyon University, Arizona
o   Harrisburg Area Community College of Pennsylvania
o   Harrisburg School of the Bible, Pennsylvania
o   Howard University
o   The University of Kansas
o   Kean College of New Jersey
o   Lehigh University of Pennsylvania
o   Lock Haven University of Pennsylvania
o   Longview Community College of Missouri
o   Mansfield University of Pennsylvania
o   McDaniel College (Western Maryland College)

Professional Careers

- o Mississippi State University
- o Missouri Western State University
- o Morehouse College of Georgia
- o North Carolina College of Theology
- o The University of North Texas
- o The University of Memphis
- o The University of Missouri, Columbia
- o The University of Missouri, Kansas City
- o The University of Pittsburgh
- o Northwest Missouri State University
- o Oral Roberts University of Oklahoma
- o Park University of Missouri
- o Pennsylvania State Police Academy, Hershey
- o Pennsylvania State University, Middletown
- o Regional Police Academy, Kansas City MO
- o Rockhurst University of Missouri
- o Sarasota School of Counseling of Florida
- o Shippensburg State University of Pennsylvania
- o Spelman College of Georgia
- o Syracuse University of New York
- o Temple University of Pennsylvania
- o The University of Utah

Cheyney University Emblem
Wikipedia

65

Dickinson College Graduate William Gumby

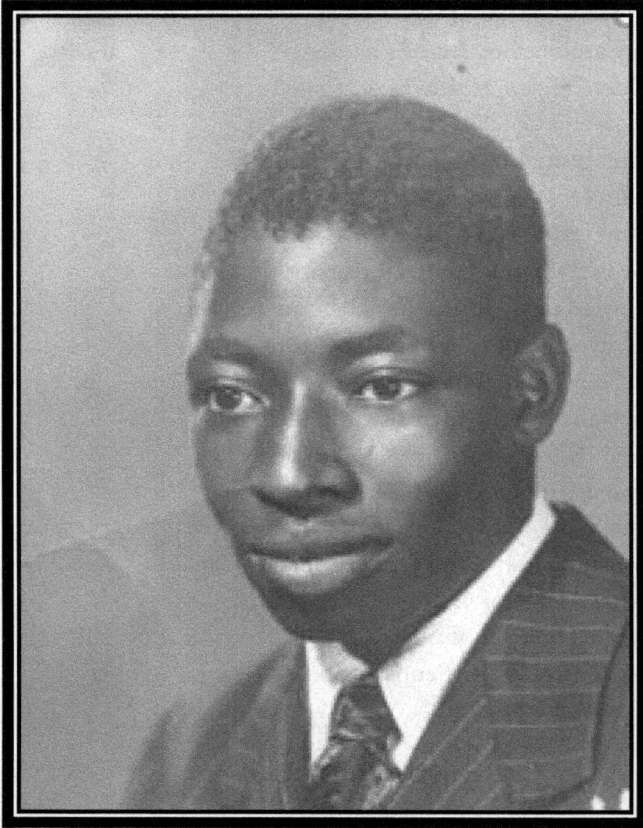

William Lynn Gumby graduated from Dickinson College of Carlisle PA. William completed his Master of Science in Chemistry at Pennsylvania State University located in State College, PA.

Courtesy of the Harry L. Gumby Family Archives

PHOTO 16. SHILOH BAPTIST OF CARLISLE PA

The Shiloh Baptist Church of Carlisle Pennsylvania is a Gumby family church of worship. One of the builders of this church was Elias Van Buren Parker, the father in-law of Harry Nelson Charles Gumby.

Google Image © 2015

Music Arts
Photo 17. Bauchum Sisters Music

Music is a family trait in the Gumby family. Loretta Ann Gumby Furman, daughter of Mary Evelyn Gumby was a vocalist. Thomas D. Gumby, son of Lucinda Gumby, played in several bands, and was a member of the vocal group, "The Concords."

Angela Denise Gumby, daughter of John W. Gumby is a musician, (piano), choir director, singer and songwriter. Angela writes poetry, and produces plays and musicals for her church; Mount Zion Missionary Baptist Church of Steelton, PA. Angela also plays the clarinet, alto saxophone, French horn, and violin.

Danielle Ashe Gumby, daughter of Angela D. Gumby is a pianist and choir director. In addition to the piano, Danielle plays the xylophone, and the marimba.

Jessica Ann Bauchum, daughter of Rosalind Gumby Bauchum is a music educator. Like her father, James, Jessica plays the piano and organ for church ministries. Jessica plays the clarinet, tenor saxophone, and guitar.

Stephanie Lorene Bauchum, daughter of Rosalind Gumby Bauchum plays the alto saxophone, piano, and is a singer. Stephanie is also an audio engineer.

Chapter 7
The Family Tree

Between 1850 and 1860, the Gumby family members moved to Cumberland County, Pennsylvania. Gumby, Parker, and other former slaves and their descendants are buried in the Mount Tabor (Colored) Cemetery in Mount Holly Springs, Lincoln Cemetery in Harrisburg, and Union Cemetery in Carlisle, PA. The first African American cemetery in Mount Holly Springs is approximately fifty yards behind the Mount Tabor church. Buried in this cemetery are Henry and Jane Johnson, and other former slave families as the Burd, Calloway, Bowman, Townsend, Wilkerson, and Jordon families.

Since the first part of the 20th century, the cemetery located behind the church has become overgrown with trees, bushes, and tall grass. A goal is to clear the brush, document graves, and preserve this earlier burial ground of former slaves.

The former cemetery is testament to the families born enslaved and freed after the Civil War. Depositions from Civil War pension applications tell the story of the lives of individuals, their lives in slavery, and their lives following emancipation.

The family tree is a comprehensive presentation of the Gumby family compiled from resources identified earlier in Chapter One. Although all branches of the Gumby family are being collected at the printing of this text, we are working to expand the collection of all branches of the family. Equally important, we acknowledge the Gumby families in Philadelphia, Johnstown, Pittsburgh, York, Reading, and Gettysburg Pennsylvania. The Gumby family extension also includes Maryland, Delaware, New York, Virginia, Ohio, Texas, Louisiana, Nevada, and other areas within the United States.

69

GUMBY FAMILY CEMETERY

Shown is a photograph of a part of the cemetery. This photo is courtesy of the Hallowed Ground Project of Pennsylvania.

PHOTO 18. MOUNT TABOR CEMETERY

The Chronology of Gumby

Since the 1600s, colonial records show the name Gumby with variation in spelling. Gombe, Gombeh, Gumby, Gumbee, Gumbey, Gumbie, Gumbo, Gunby, Grumby, Cumbo, and Combo are found in various documents. This chapter presents the Gumby family story.

1619 – The first Africans arrive in the British Colonies, Pointe Comfort, Virginia.

1655 – Gumby age fifty, appears in the property inventory of William Brocas. Included on the list are other slaves with each person's age and health status. Gumby, born in 1605 later becomes a slave of John Carter of Corotomon Plantation, Virginia.

1659 – Lillely, Jacke, and Gumby delivered to Christ Church Parrish, Barbados.

1680–Tom Gumby, an African is born. The year 1680 is based upon information Tom (Dadda) Gumby told Phillip Vickers Fithian at Nomini Hall in 1774. Tom Gumby is 94-years old, and Fithian includes this fact in his diary. Tom was referred to as the patriarch of many of the slaves living at Nomini Hall.

1700–The estimate birth of the "Gumby" listed in the 1775 inventory list of *White and Blacks at Nomony Hall*. This individual is believed to be Tom Gumby, perhaps the son of Tom "Dadda" Gumby.

1720 – The birth year of Dick Gumby, son of Tom and Kate Gumby.

1721 – The birth of Jack Gumby who is noted as fifty-four years old in the Nomini Hall Inventory of Whites and Blacks in 1775 Westmoreland County, Virginia.[23]

1724 - Robert King Carter identifies Tom Gumby in his letters and papers. An entry reports Carter sent his slave Tom Gumby to deliver a letter to a friend Captain John Steptoe; *"I sent away a great many Letters by T Gumby to Mr. Steptoe."* (Captain John Steptoe).

1726 – 1732 The first reference to a brother of Tom Gumby in a Will of Robert King Carter. Tom's brother is David.

1727 - The birth of Dick Gumby listed in the *Inventory of Whites and Black at Nomini Hall in 1775*. Dick is shown as a "joiner" in the Nomini Hall 1775 Inventory. Listed next to Dick is Nelson Gumby, a "joiner," at the age of thirty-two.

1732 – The estimated birth of Martha Gumby, daughter of Tom and Kate Gumby. The birth of Robbin Gumby is recorded in 1732. Robin is shown in the 1775 Nomini Hall inventory. Robert Carter III identified Robin Gumby in the Gift of Deed. Robin married Sukey Spence and was later identified as Robin Spence.

1733 - Old Gumby and his wife Martha appear in Robert King Carter's 1733 inventory list of slaves. Included with Old Gumby and Martha is their son, a young man named Jack[24]. Listed in this same 1733 slave inventory are Thomas Gumby his wife Kate, and their children Mary, Dick, 13-years old and a one-year old baby named Martha. One could conclude that "Old Gumby" and his wife Martha were possibly the parents of Tom Gumby.

1736 – Jack Gumby is born. Jack is identified as thirty-nine years of age in the 1775 Nomini Hal Inventory, and is noted as a Blacksmith.

1738 – The birth of Joan Gumby. Joan later has three daughters; Sarah (the mother of Gabriel and Dilse), Barbara Gumby Newman (the mother of James), and Henney Wells (the mother of Levina, Prince, and Molly)[25].

1746 – The birth year of John Gumby, the son of Jack Gumby as shown in the 1775 Nomini Hall *Inventory of Whites and Black* residents.

1750 – 1760, the possible range of time of the birth of Thomas Gumby shown in the 1830 Census of Frederick County, VA. The Census was in the Eastern District of Frederick County. (Washington DC: National Archives and Records Administration)

1754 – The birth of Willoughby (Willoby) Gumby.

1756 – Birth year of Nelson Gumby, joiner for Robert Carter III, of Nomini Hall.

1760 – Jack Gumby was born in 1760. Jack is a possible great-grandson of Old Gumby or perhaps the grandson of the "Jack" listed in the 1733 inventory only as "a young man."

1760 - The birth year of Katy Gumby, shown in the 1850 census of Loudoun County, Virginia.

1761 – The birth year of Nelson Gumby who is shown as fourteen years of age in the 1775 list of *Whites and Black at Nomini Hall Plantation.*

1762 – The birth year of John Gumby, the son of Jack Gumby.

1767 - The inventory of slave owner Willoughby Newton of Westmoreland County, VA shows a slave named "Gumby" valued at fifty dollars. There is not a first name to identify this Gumby individual. (Westmoreland County Records and Inventories, 1767 - 1776)

1767 - Nelson Gumby, a slave of Robert Carter III is born. Manumission records show Nelson as 24 years old in 1791 when the document was drafted. Rachel Gumby, the wife of Nelson was born around 1766. The same records list Rachel as 25 years old.

1774 - Records of Phillip Vickers Fithian show "Dadda" Gumby as 94 years old upon Fithian's arrival at Nomini Hall. If Dadda Gumby were 94 years in 1774, he would have been born in or around 1680.

1775 - *Census of Whites and Blacks* conducted at Nomini Hall. One entry shows "Gumby" at 75-years old. The Gumby shown first under the list of Black Males may be a son of the ninety-four-year old Tom "Dadda" Gumby. Additionally, listed are David, age sixty-four, Solomon, age twenty-six, Dick age forty-nine, and Ignatius, age fourteen.

1790 – The death of Kate Gumby, wife of Tom Gumby. Tom Gumby may have died between the years of 1775 and 1782.[26]

1791–Robert Carter III files the Deed of Gift freeing 509 slaves. The Gumby slaves freed initially were; Abby Gumby, Clouden Gumby, Dorcas Gumby, Frances Gumby, Humphrey Gumby, Joan Gumby, John Gumby, Sarah Gumby, Thomas Gumby, and Willoby Gumby.

Nelson and Rachel Gumby have a baby boy named Nelson Gumby in **1791**.

1793 – Nelson and Rachel Gumby give birth to Willoby Gumby.

1794–Nelson and Rachel Gumby are freed January 1, 1794. Nelson was estimated to be thirty-five years old when manumitted.

1795 – Nelson and Rachel Gumby give birth to a daughter, Haney Gumby.

1800 - The first-year Gumby family members pay taxes following slavery. Willoughby Gumby shows one (1) tithe and one slave in his Westmoreland County, Virginia household over the age of sixteen. (Heinegg, Westmoreland County Personal Property Tax List, 1782 - 1815)

1803 - The Frederick County, VA Tax list shows John Gumby and his wife Diannah paying taxes in 1803 and for several years afterwards. John and Diannah's sons Tom and John Jr., are listed in succeeding tax years. Nelson Gumby and his wife Rachel are also shown on the 1803 tax list.

1806—Samboe Gumby is listed in the Westmoreland County, lower district tax list as paying one tithe.

1810 - This census of Frederick County confirms John Gumby as a free man. John Gumby had nine family members living with him at the time of the census.

Rachel Gumby is shown as a free woman, with five others residing with her in Frederick County. Elijah Gumby was born in 1810 in Virginia. Other persons in the house may have been Nelson, Joan, Richard (Dick), James and Haney.

1812—There is one data source showing 1812 as the birth of Nelson Gumby. Other Census information show the date of 1819.

1813 - Westmoreland County, VA Tax List In 1813, The following Gumby members were shown as Free Negroes; Sarah Gumbey, 2 tithes, Joanna Gumbey, 1 tithe, Betsey Gumbey, 1 tithe and Rose Gumbey, 1 tithe.

1817 - Thomas Gumby was born in 1817. Thomas is located in the 1830 Census in Eastern Frederick County, the 1840 census in Shenandoah County and the 1850 census in Warren County, Virginia.

1819 – The birth of Nelson Gumby as indicated in the 1850 Frederick County, 1860 Warren County, Virginia, and the 1870 Cumberland County, Pennsylvania Census.

1850 - The 1850 Census of Loudoun County, Virginia shows Jack and Kate Gumby. Both Jack and Kate at the age of ninety would have been born around 1760. There is a man named Jack living at Cancer Plantation in Prince William County shown as 33 years old in 1791. The age listing shown for Jack Gumby in Loudoun may indicate the same person.

1860 – Nelson and Sarah Jane Gumby appear on the Frederick County, Virginia Census. The family also appear on Warren County's Virginia's Free Inhabitants Census.

1870 – Nelson, Jane, Catherine, and Edward Gumby appear on the Census for Cumberland County, PA.

1879 - Elijah (Eli) Gumby dies during July 1879 at the age of twenty-one. Elijah's death was reported on the Dickinson Township Death Report ending May 1880. (1850-1880)

1880 - Jane S. and her four children; Elizabeth, James, John, and Charles, appear on the Census. Grandchildren John, Sarah J., and Julian are listed in the household.

1897 – April 13, 1897 Samuel D. Gumby, son of Nelson and Sarah Jane Newman Gumby marries Annie Stackfield.

1898 – January 6, Charles Edward Gumby marries Mary Bowers.

1900 – John H. Gumby, son of Nelson and Sarah Jane Gumby dies in Barnitz (Cumberland County) Pennsylvania.

Chronology Observations

Four hundred and sixty Africans named Gumby lived in Virginia between 1840 and 1865. Notably, two individuals, Nelson Gumby born in 1791 and the Nelson born in either 1812,[27] or 1819 (varying dates) were named after the Nelson Gumby freed by Robert Carter III. It is important to note many slaves were named after parents, grandparents, aunts, uncles and other family members.[28]

Census records for Frederick County, Virginia show the births of Elijah Gumby born in 1810, John Gumby Jr., born in 1815, James Gumby's birth in 1818 and Nelson Gumby born in 1819. Tom and John Gumby Jr., are the sons of John Gumby as shown on the tax records. The tax list shows Richard (Dick) in the house with his mother Rachel in 1813.

Nelson Gumby born in 1767, married Rachel born in 1765. Nelson and Rachel were the parents of Joan (Jone) born in 1784, Dick born in 1788, James born in 1790, Nelson[x2] born in 1791, Willoby born in 1793, and Haney, born in 1795. John Gumby, and Nelson and Rachel Gumby are indicated as Carter's free Negroes residing in Fredrick County, Virginia on the 1800 tax list.

Nelson Gumby, the son of Nelson and Rachel Gumby born in 1791, may be the father of Nelson[x3] born in 1819. If Nelson were born in 1812 as some records report, his father Nelson[x2] would have been twenty-one years old. If born in 1819, Nelson's father would have been twenty-eight years old. The name of the mother of the third Nelson born in 1819 is unknown.

Nelson[x3] Gumby, born in Virginia in 1819, married Sarah Jane Newman, born in Frederick County, Virginia in 1820. Nelson and Sarah Jane Nelson Gumby and Sarah Jane Newman Gumby gave birth to the following children;

- Mary Gumby, a daughter born in Virginia in 1843.
- James Gumby, a son born in Virginia in 1845 (could not find a record of marriage or children).
- Elijah Gumby, a son born in Virginia in 1846.
- John Henry Nelson Gumby, a son born in Virginia in 1848. (Died April 1900).
- Evaline Gumby, a daughter born in Virginia in 1850.
- Samuel D. Gumby, a son born in Virginia in 1851 (married Annie L. Stackfield, born in 1859).
- Jacob Gumby, a son born in Virginia in 1853 (no record of marriage or children).
- Charles Edward Gumby, a son born in Virginia in 1859. (married Mary Bowers, January 6, 1898).[29]
- Eli Gumby, a male born in 1858 in Virginia.
- Sarah Gumby, a female born in Virginia in 1859.

Gumby Information Sources

NEWSPAPER 1 CHARLES EDWARD GUMBY

Charles Edward Gumby the son of Nelson and Sarah Jane Gumby was born in 1868 in Barnitz, PA. Charles, known as "Ed" married Emma Bowers. Charles and Emma Bowers lived in Mount Holly Springs. The 1900 Census shows Charles and Emma on the day of the Census with Harry and Elsie Gumby in the house.

> Charles Edward Weakly Gumby, 55 Baltimore street, Mt. Holly Springs, died at his home. Mr. Gumby, a native of Barnitz, was 76 years old and a member of the A. M. E. Zion church in Carlisle. He is survived by his wife, Mrs. Mary E. Bowers Gumby. Services were held on Tuesday with burial in Union Cemetery.

The newspaper announcement of the death of Charles Edward Gumby shows the name of "Weakly," as a second middle name.

COMET NEWS, EAST BERLIN, PA SEPTEMBER 27, 1946

The Certificate of Registration for Nelson Gumby, Warren County, Virginia, May 17, 1852

All free slaves registered with the court in the area of their residence. An 1806 law mandated anyone who became free after 1806 had to register, or move from the state of Virginia. Nelson Gumby registered May 17, 1852 in Warren, Virginia.

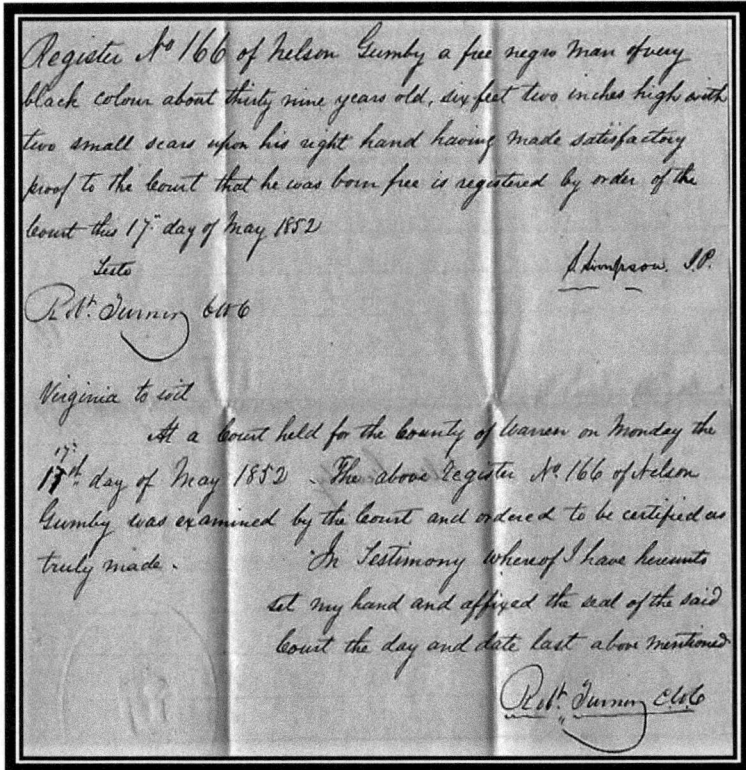

DOCUMENT 10. NELSON GUMBY'S FREE REGISTRATION PAPER

Source Library of Virginia

DOCUMENT 11. MARRIAGE APPLICATION FOR CHARLES EDWARD AND MARY EMMA BOWERS

Charles Edward Weakly Gumby and Mary E. Bowers applied for a marriage license in Cumberland County, PA. Charles was the son of Nelson Gumby. According to information from the 1910 Census for Mount Holly Springs PA, Charles and Mary resided near families with the surname of Cole, Bowman, Talton, James, Curtis, Johnson, Burd, Howard, Wilkerson, and Calloway.

Source – Familysearch.org

The death certificate for Samuel Gumby Nelson. and Jane Gumby as his parents. The certificate shows Virginia as the birth state for both parents.

Source – Familysearch.org

The obituary announcement of the death of Samuel Gumby.

SAMUEL GUMBY

Funeral services for Samuel Gumby, 1002 Fox street, who died Thursday at his home will be held Monday afternoon at 2 o'clock at the Charles W. Curtis funeral parlors, 1000 North Sixth street, with the Rev. W. J. Winfield, pastor of the Monroe Street Church of God, assisted by the Rev. Mr. Queen of the Bethel A. M. E. Church, Carlisle, officiating. Burial will be in the Lincoln Cemetery. The body may be viewed at the funeral parlors, Sunday from 4 to 10 p. m.

He is survived by two daughters, Mrs. Robert Curtis, and Miss Alice Gumby, both of Harrisburg; a son, William Gumby, Harrisburg, a brother, Edward Gumby, Carlisle; eight grandchildren and four great-grandchildren.

Harrisburg Telegraph, October 23, 1937,
Source–Newspaper.com

NEWSPAPER 2 OBITUARY OF SAMUEL GUMBY

Annie Stackfield Gumby

DEATHS AND FUNERALS

MRS. ANNA GUMBY

Funeral service will be held Tuesday afternoon at 2 o'clock in the Monroe Street Church of God for Mrs. Anna Gumby, 56, wife of Samuel Gumby, who died yesterday in her home, 1148 Cumberland street, following a heart attack. Two daughters, Mrs. Jane Curtis and Miss Alice Gumby; two sons, William and Enos Gumby; six grandchildren and two great grandchildren survive. The Rev. W. J. Winfield will officiate, and burial will be in the Lincoln cemetery.

The death announcement of Mrs. Anna Stackfield Gumby, wife of Samuel Gumby. **Source: Harrisburg Telegraph, July 24, 1926.**

NEWSPAPER 3 OBITUARY OF ANNA GUMBY

John Henry Nelson Gumby (son of Nelson Gumby and Sarah Gumby) married Rachel Ellen Simms (Gumby). Rachel, the daughter of Charles Sims, was born in 1866 in Pennsylvania and died in 1942 in Carlisle. **Source: Gettysburg Times, November 6, 1942**

Mrs. Rachel Ellen Gumby

Mrs. Rachel E. Gumby died at the home of her daughter, Miss Elsie Gumby, Carlisle.

She is survived by two sons, Harry, Mt. Holly Springs, and George, Carlisle; two other daughters, Rachel Arter, Carlisle, and Mary Simms, Philadelphia; two sisters, Mrs. Lucinda Williams and Mrs. Annie Moser, both of Gettysburg; 23 grandchildren, 4 great-grandchildren and a number of nieces and nephews.

Services will be held Saturday afternoon at 2:30 o'clock in the West Street A. M. E. Zion church of which she was a member. The pastor, the Rev. H. N. Drew, will officiate. Burial will be in Union cemetery, Carlisle.

John Gumby and Rachel Simms Gumby were parents of the following children; Elsie Gumby, George Gumby, Harry N. C. Gumby, Jacob Gumby, Lyle Gumby, James Gumby, Lucinda Gumby, Mary Gumby, and Rachel Gumby.

Harry Nelson Charles Gumby was born 1892 in Barnitz, Cumberland County, Pennsylvania and is buried in Mount Tabor Cemetery in Mount Holly Springs, Pennsylvania.

Photo - Find A Grave

Lucinda Gumby, the daughter of John and Rachel Ellen Gumby had five children. Their names were William Gumby, Charles Gumby, Marian Gumby, Marcus Gumby, Betty Gumby Jordan, and Elsie Mae Gumby.

William Gumby, the son of Lucinda married Shirley Figueroa. The couple had one daughter Suzan.

Marcus E. Gumby, the son of Lucinda Gumby had one son, Marcus E. Gumby Jr.

Charles R. Gumby, the son of Lucinda Gumby had a son with Deloris Washington, Charles R. Washington Jr., Charles R. Gumby was also the father of Duane Coleman.

Betty Gumby, the daughter of Lucinda Gumby married Edward Giles. The couple had four children; Henry Giles, Mary Giles Baltimore, Dennis L. Giles and Linda Giles Lawrence. Betty died August 7, 1986.

Marian Gumby, and James Eastman had two children, Jocelyn Eastman, and Leslie Eastman. Elsie Mae Gumby gave birth to one son, Dana Maurice Gumby

Gumby, Owens

Elsie M. Gumby was born April 26, 1894 in Pennsylvania. Elsie died September 15, 1994. Elsie Gumby's grave is in Union Cemetery, Carlisle, Pennsylvania.

Elsie Gumby and Minister Jesse Talbert had a daughter Sarah Elizabeth Gumby. Sarah E. Gumby, the daughter of Elsie Gumby and Jesse Talbert gave birth to two sons with Benjamin M. Owens; Robert Lathaire Owens and Donald Ellsworth Owens.

Robert L. Owens, the son of Sarah E. Gumby and Benjamin Myoli Owens had the following children; Jeffery L. Kirkland, Robert L. Thomas, and Elizabeth M. Owens. Robert L. Owens later married Geraldine Owens. Tabitha Owens Banks was born to the union of Robert and Geraldine Owens.

Jeffrey Lynn Kirkland, and Shirley Rosco gave birth to Valesha Marquette Kirkland, Rashaad Jamel Kirkland, Malik Ahmad Kirkland, and Saleem Lateef Kirkland.

Valesha Kirkland and Jordan Richardson became the parents of two children; Jordan Richardson II, and Jada Richardson.

Robert Lathaire Thomas had a son Gregory Allen Walker. Elizabeth Marie Owens, the daughter of Robert L. Owens Sr., had a son, Brian Lewis Owens. Antoinette Elizabeth Williams was born to Elizabeth and Anthony Williams.

Tabitha Owens married Charles Edward Banks. The couple became parents of Morgan Elizabeth Banks, Nicole Erica Banks, and Meredith Alexandria Banks.

Donald E. Owens, the son of Sarah E. Gumby and Benjamin Myoli Owens married Isabel Green. This union included; William H. Owens (Marsha), Albert D. Owens (Guale), Donald E. Owens, Harriet A. Hodge, Sarah E. Horn, Donna M. Daughtry, Emma Carothers (Charles), Roxane Creamer, and Cheryl A. Knight (Lesman).

Harriet A., the daughter of Donald E. and Isabel Owens married Elmer Hodge. Born from this union was Darryl Hodge.

William, the son of Donald and Isabel, married Marsha Johnson. The couple became parents of Anthony Wright, Perry Owens, Stacy Owens, Ruth Ann Owens, Michael Owens, and William Owens.

Albert David (Albie) (dec'd), the son of Donald and Isabel Owens married Guale. The couple had two children; Christopher Owens, and Raya Owens.

Sarah E., the daughter of Donald and Isabel Owens, married William Horn. The couple had two daughters, Nichole Horn and Aleya Horn.

Donald Owens Jr. had a daughter LaDawn Owens. Donna Mae Owens, the daughter of Donald Owens and Isabel Owens married William Daughtry. William Daughtry Jr., was born from this union.

Emma Owens, the daughter of Donald and Isabel Owens, married Charles Carrothers. From this union were Danielle, Rachel, Charles, Edward, Mark, and Emily Carrothers.

Roxann M. Owens, the daughter of Donald and Isabel Owens married Thomas Cremer (dec'd). The couple gave birth to Andrea, Kent, Kingsley and Antoinette Creamer.

Carl Lathaire Owens., (dec'd) the son of Donald and Isabel Owens married Renita, and became parents of Carlita R. (Eggleston), Dyan S., and Joseph P. Owens.

Cheryl Owens, the daughter of Donald and Isabel Owens married Lesman Knight. The couple has three children Lesman Jr., Ashley, and Benjamin Knight.

George Gumby, the son of John H. Gumby and Rachel E. Simms Gumby was born in 1896 in Pennsylvania. George died February 2, 1955 in Carlisle, Pennsylvania. George Gumby is buried in Union Cemetery of Carlisle, PA. George had one son; Melvin Hinton.

Lila Jane (Lyle) Gumby, the daughter of John H. Gumby and Rachel E. Simms Gumby was born June 1897 in Pennsylvania. Lila and William Russ had one son, William Russ Jr

Gumby, Arter

Rachel Gumby was born April 18, 1907 in Pennsylvania. Rachel died December 4, 2004. Rachel E. Gumby, the daughter of John Gumby and Rachel Gumby married George P. Arter, (born in 1906 the son of George W. Arter) on September 1, 1926. George and Rachel had eight children:

Richard Arter, born in 1925, Carl E. Arter dec'd, born August 26, 1927, died October 27, 1988, Jean E. Arter (Carter), born in 1931. Jean married Barney Carter, and gave birth to Scott Carter, Candace Carter, Chrystal Carter, Penny Carter, and Jordon Carter. George P. Arter Jr., was born in 1933. George Arter married Mae and to this union seven children were born; George, Derick, Rita, Jennifer, Sandy, Caron and Trinna Arter.

Delores A. (Sue) Arter, the daughter of George and Rachel Arter was born May 4, 1935. Delores died June 10, 2011. Delores had three children, Steven, Marsha, and Jodie. Julia A. Arter (Doleman) dec'd, born in 1940, died in 2007. Julia and Joseph Doleman had the following children; Johnnie, Monica, Joyce, and Keith Doleman.

Earl W. Arter, the son of George and Rachel Arter was born in 1937. Earl died November 28, 2015. Earl married Barbara Goens. Tarren and Earl Jr., were born to the union. Rachel Arter (Tanner) born in 1943, married William Tanner and they had two children; Troy and Shawn Tanner.

Lucinda L. Gumby was born in 1901 in Pennsylvania. The 1930 census reports Lucinda as a stepdaughter living in the household. Others in the house were Mary Gumby, James Gumby, and Jacob Gumby.

African Americans previously lived in households with large numbers of family members. The Gumby and Arter household in Carlisle included several generations of family members ranging from the mother, daughter, grandchildren, great-grandchildren, great-great grandchildren, and in-laws. The Gumby-Arter household accommodated this large family by acquiring two joined housing units and cutting a door through the wall to make one home. The 1940 Census listed Rachel Ellen Gumby as the head of the home.

DOCUMENT 12 - 1940 PENNSYLVANIA CENSUS

Source – 1940 Decennial Census, Cumberland County, PA

The Grave of George and Rachel E. Arter

Photo - Find A Grave

**Earl Warren Arter, Sr.
Son of George and Rachel E. Arter**

The Family of Samuel D. Gumby
and
Annie L. Stackfield Gumby

Samuel D. Gumby (son of Nelson Gumby and Sarah Gumby) married Annie L. Stackfield (born February 1859), on April 13, 1897. Annie was the daughter of Michael Stackfield. Samuel and Annie became parents of; Jane Gumby, born in 1886, William Gumby, born April 1893, Enos Gumby, born November 1897, and Alice Gumby, born in May 1891.

Jane Gumby, the daughter of Samuel Gumby and Annie Stackfield Gumby married Robert Curtis (born in 1878) on November 23, 1899. (Pennsylvania Marriages, 1709-1940," (https://familysearch.org/ark:/61903/1:1:V26Z-4YL :)

Robert and Jane Curtis became parent of the following children; Dorothy Curtis (born 1903), Robert S. Curtis, (born 1905), John Curtis (born 1907), Floyd Curtis (born 1920), Earl Curtis (born 1924), and Orvin Curtis (born 1929). Robert Jr., married Ruth McGowan (born 1907), April 5, 1930; Ruth was the daughter of Ausburn McGowan and Emma Thompson.

Alice Gumby, the daughter of Samuel and Annie Stackfield Gumby had one daughter; Naomi Gumby.

1900 Census of Samuel Gumby Family, Harrisburg, PA

The Gumby, Jackson, Grayson, Wilkerson, Curtis, Manigault Connection

Elizabeth Gumby, the daughter of Nelson and Sarah Jane Gumby married George W. Jackson, a Civil War veteran of the 127th United States Colored Regiment. Elizabeth and George gave birth to a daughter, Julia Jackson. Elizabeth's second marriage was to Samuel Greason, (also spelled Grayson), and to this union two children were born; Sarah Jane Greason and John T. Greason.

Family history shows Julia Jackson, the daughter of George and Elizabeth Gumby Jackson, married a man with the surname of Gray. There is no record of any children born to this union.

Greason, Wilkerson, Curtis, James, Buck, Starkes

Sarah Jane Greason, the daughter of Elizabeth Gumby Greason; married a Wilkerson (first marriage). Under this union, Kenneth Wilkerson was born. Sarah Jane Greason later married Robert S. Curtis. In the second marriage, Jane had two children; Lydia Curtis and Mary Curtis. Sarah Jane Greason then married John James (third marriage), through this union Chester Ray James (born 1897) and Lewis James were born.

Chester Ray James, son of Sarah Jane Greason James, and John James married Annabell Prunty on May 26, 1923.[30] Chester James became the father of a daughter Grace James, and a son, Alan Miller. Lewis James, became the father of eight children; Jane (Covington) James, Lewis James Jr., William James, Ruth Mae James, Marie James, Skippie James, Harry James, and George James.

John T. Greason, the son of Elizabeth Gumby and Samuel Greason, married Virginia Harrison on October 8, 1917. Eight children were born; Dora Greason (born 1899), Beulah Greason (born 1906), Alma Greason (born 1908), Gertrude Greason, Albert I. Greason (born 1894), Constance Ellamae Greason (born 1910), Charles E. Greason (born 1892), and Hester Greason.

Dora Greason, the daughter of John T. and Virginia Harrison Greason married Clarence Buck on October 8, 1917. Born to the union of Dora and Clarence Buck were three children; Charles Buck (born 1917), (United States Census, 1930, database with images), Clarence Buck Jr., (born 1921) and William Buck (born 1922).

Lydia Curtis, the daughter of Jane Greason, married Thomas Parker. The couple had one daughter Alice J. Parker, (born 1911). Alice J. Parker married Evie Starkes on June 5, 1924. Evie and Alice became parents of Donald E. Starkes, born in 1924, and Annabelle Starkes (born 1927).

Evie Starkes died in August 1930. Later, Alice married Henry Lewis (born 1910) on December 22, 1934. (Pennsylvania, County Marriages, 1885-1950, data base with images).

Donald E. Starkes married Eula, and they had a family of ten children; Gwendolyn Starkes (Griffin), Charles Starkes, Doris Starkes (Logan), Donald E. Starkes Jr., Beverly Starkes, Joyce Starkes (Huddleston), Vonda Starkes, Richard Starkes, Edward Starkes, Vincent Starkes, Tina Starkes, Bertha Starkes (United States, GenealogyBank Obituaries, 1980-2014," database with images). Donald Starkes died July 7, 1998.

Annabelle married a man with the surname of Pitts, and later became an Anderson. Annabelle had five children; Emily Anderson, Alice Anderson, Charles Anderson, Brenda Anderson, and Darlene Anderson

Greason, Moody, Anderson

Alma Greason, the daughter of John T. and Virginia Harrison Greason (born 1908) married Eugene Moody (born 1895). Born to this union were George Moody (born 1936) (1. Census) and Gladys Moody (born 1934).

Gertrude Greason, the daughter of John T. and Virginia Harrison Greason married Harry Anderson. To this union arrived seven children; Sylvester Anderson, Walter Anderson, Mary Anderson, Charles Anderson, Harry Anderson Jr., Magdaline Anderson (born 1925), and Augustus Anderson. Magdaline Anderson married Robert Thompson.

Manigault, Tumey, Milburn, Bass, Warder

Beulah T. Greason, the daughter of John T. and Virginia Harrison Greason married Joseph F. Manigault (born 1901). Joseph F. and Beulah Manigault had seven children; John Joseph Manigault (born 1933), Ora V. Manigault (born 1935), Beulah

Manigault (born 1937), Leonard Manigault (born 1938), Viola E. Manigault (born 1940), George S. Manigault (born 1942), Geraldine O. Manigault (born 1945), (United States, GenealogyBank Obituaries, 1980-2014)

John Joseph Manigault, the son of Joseph F. and Beulah Manigault was the father of seven children; Denise Manigault, Joann Manigault, Joy Manigault, Johnathan Manigault, John Manigault, Monica Manigault, and Lisa Manigault.

Leonard E. Manigault, the son of Joseph F. and Beulah Manigault married Anna Mae Tumey (born 1938). This marriage joined Lawrence Tumey and Lutrica Tumey.

Viola Manigault, the daughter of Joseph F. and Beulah Manigault married Fabian Milburn. The couple had two children; Rhonda Milburn, and Fabian Milburn, Jr.

Beulah C. Manigault, the daughter of Joseph F. and Beulah Manigault married LeRoy Bass. The couple had two children; Dwayne S. Bass and Joseph T. Bass.

Ora V. Manigault, the daughter of Joseph F. and Beulah Manigault married Theodore Bass. Ora and Theodore gave birth to three children; Constance Bass Blake, Valarie Bass, and Daryl Bass.

Geraldine O. Manigault, the daughter of Joseph F. and Beulah Manigault married Eugene Warden. Eugene and Geraldine had one son David Warden.

Cuff, Spraglin

Mary Curtis married Frank Cuff (born 1889). From this union three children were born; William E. Cuff (born 1909), Sarah (born 1916), and Francis Cuff (born 1920). The 1910 Census of Cumberland County, PA, shows Samuel Gumby living in the household of Frank and Mary Cuff in Carlisle Pennsylvania.

Sarah Cuff married Sidney Spraglin, (Born February 4, 1891), and to this union three children were born; William Spraglin, Margaret Spraglin, and Shirley Spraglin. William Spraglin married Carolyn Wells, (born 1934) and to this union two children were born; Ricardo Spraglin, and David Spraglin.

Marjorie Spraglin married a Cheeks and later married a Lewis. Shirley Spraglin married a Thomas and had three children; Sherrie Thomas, Daryl Thomas, and Anthony Thomas. Later, Shirley married a man with the surname of Knothe.

Wilkerson, Bird

Kenneth Wilkerson, married Rachel Bird and from this union were the following offspring; Marion E. Wilkerson, Rachael Wilkerson, John Richard Wilkerson, Clarence Wilkerson, Warren Reed Wilkerson, Andrew Davis, Richard Davis, and Monecia Renee Spraglin (Clary).

Clarence Wilkerson (born 1915), the son of Kenneth and Rachel Bird Wilkerson married Bessie Stripling (born 1917) and their children were; Clarence Wilkerson Jr., Jean Wilkerson, Kenneth Wilkerson, Rachael Mae Calloway, John Wilkerson, Kathleen Wilkerson, James Wilkerson, Margaret Wilkerson, Joan Wilkerson, William Wilkerson. Rachael Wilkerson, the daughter of Kenneth and Rachel Wilkerson gave birth to Donald Calloway.

John Richard Wilkerson, (born December 10, 1945) the son of Kenneth and Rachel Wilkerson, married Helen M. Wright. The names of their children were; Dora C. Mary Wilkerson, Marilyn Wilkerson (Brown), Stanley Wilkerson, Anna Wilkerson (DuBois), and Chubbie Wilkerson.

Author Note: I am indebted to the late Robert Lathaire Owens, the son of Sarah Elizabeth Gumby. Robert Lathaire Owens and I compared family history notes on one of his visits to the Midwest with his wife, Geraldine. Robert had a list of names of various branches of the family. I consulted secondary genealogy data resources to gather, birth, death, marriage, and military information to present this section of family history.

The Family of
William H. Gumby and Anna E. Courts Gumby

William Henry Gumby Sr., (born April 2, 1884, died June 30, 1958). William, the son of Samuel D. Gumby and Annie Stackfield Gumby, married Anna Elizabeth Courts (born December 21, 1907) Anna Elizabeth died January 13, 2004.

William Gumby and Anna Courts Gumby gave birth to the following children: Pauline E. Gumby, born on July 9, 1928, (died October 16, 2007); Vivian Anna Gumby Murray, born June 9,1932, (died on June 15, 2003); William Henry Gumby Jr., born June 14, 1935, (died on April 1, 2012); Ronald E. Gumby, Robert W. Gumby, Charles Edward Gumby, and John Wesley Gumby.

The William and Anna Courts Gumby family lived and raised their family in Harrisburg, Dauphin County, Pennsylvania. The family lived in the Capital area of Harrisburg which was a very vibrant community of churches, schools, civic, social, and fraternal organizations, businesses and commerce.

The Gumby family worshipped at the Monroe Street Church of God, and the Bethel African Methodist Episcopal Church. The Gumby children attended the Downey School, and later upon integration; the Woodward School.

Photograph by Jeffry Sanders

Vivian Anna Gumby, the daughter of William and Anna Elizabeth Gumby gave birth to the following children; Richard Lester Gumby, Michael Murray, (dec'd), Solomon Murray Jr., Steven Murray, Thomas Murray (dec'd May 22, 2012), Patricia Copeland, China Murray Buie, Sandra Murray Corbett, and Angela Murray.

Naomi Ruth Gumby Banks, and Esterman Ross had the following children; Charles W. Banks (Brenda), Ronald B. Banks (Linda), and Gail Ross.

Wendell S. Banks Sr. became the father of following children; Loretta Banks, Wendell S. Banks Jr., Charles A. Banks, and Arnold Banks (dec'd).

Photo by Find A Grave, #48442041

Reba I. Banks Geary the daughter of Naomi Ruth Banks gave birth to; Barbara Banks Stewart (dec'd), and Robert (Butch) Banks.

Charles W. Banks, the son of Naomi Ruth Gumby Banks, had one daughter, Crystal Banks.

Ronald Banks became the father of Lisa Banks, Ronald Banks Jr., Tony Banks, Nicole Banks, Monica Banks, and Jaimie Beisel-Banks.

William Henry Gumby Jr., was the father of Lynda Gumby (dec'd), Laura Gumby Winslow, Deloris Gumby, Gloria Gumby (dec'd), and William Henry Gumby III.

Charles Edward Gumby, the son of William H. and Anna Elizabeth Gumby did not have children.

Robert Walter Gumby married Bernice Watson, and became parents of; Darrell Edward Gumby, and Jerry Walter Gumby. Darrell Edward passed June 18, 2007.

Ronald Eugene Gumby became the father of Ronald Eugene Gumby Jr., Carol Ann Gumby Henderson, Renee Gumby Colbert, Crystal Gumby, Candice Ingram Gumby, Linda Green Baltimore Gumby, and Jeremiah Gumby Holmes.

Ronald E. Gumby Jr., the son of Ronald E. Gumby Sr., married Jeanette Summers. Together they are the parents of three children; Nickki Weyant, JaRonda Gumby, and JaKia Gumby.

Carol Ann Gumby, the daughter of Ronald E. Gumby married Charles Henderson. The couple had four children; Janiece, Janelle, Christopher, and Charles Henderson.

Janiece did not have children. Janelle gave birth to two children, Reginald Alexander, and Jacqueline Henderson. Charles married Chinnelle Harris and both of them became the parents of Chase Henderson, Chance Henderson, Karaqyn Harris and Nevah Harris. Christopher had one daughter; Lauryn Henderson.

Renee Gumby, the daughter of Ronald E. Gumby married Samuel Colbert. They are the parents of Samuel G..Colbert Jr. Samuel Colbert Jr., had two children; a daughter Anijah, and a son, Samuel A. Colbert.

Crystal Gumby, the daughter of Ronald E. Gumby gave birth to Collier Gumby. Collier the son of Crystal Gumby became the the father of Jasken Gumby-Rickard, Nikaya Gumby-Rickard, and Raven Gumby-Rickard.

Candace Ingram Gumby gave birth to Lechelle Smith, and Natalie Terrell. Leshelle gave birth to twins, Nasir (dec'd), and Jalen Smith. Natalie gave birth to one child, Andre Terrell.

Linda Marie Baltimore Green Gumby adopted three children; daughters Monica Ivy, Inez Crowner, and a son Jamal Cottman. Inez had a daughter Ana Crowner.

John Wesley Gumby married Carol A. Mounds. The couple had two children; Angela Denise Gumby, and John Wesley Gumby Jr. Angela, the daughter of John Wesley, and Carol A. Mounds Gumby gave birth to two children; a daughter, Danielle Ashe Gumby, and a son, Napier Monroe Gumby.

John Wesley Gumby Jr., the son of John Wesley and Carol A. Mounds Gumby had one daughter; LaJonda Gumby. The marriage of John and Carol Mounds Gumby later dissolved.
John Wesley Gumby later married Sandra M. Johnson.

Photo by Jeffry Sanders
Courtesy of John Wesley Gumby Archive

Photo 19 Sons and grandson of William H. Gumby

The sons of William H. Gumby Sr., are shown in a family photograph. Shown from the left are Elder Dr. John W. Gumby Sr., William H. Gumby, Jr., Ronald E. Gumby, Elder Robert W. Gumby, Charles E. Gumby. Seated is Richard W. Gumby.

Gumby-Murray

Thomas M. Murray son of Vivian Murray, and Thomas Henry Davis gave birth to the following children: Thomas Murray Jr., Tanisha Murray, dec'd (February 1, 2016), TyShawn Murray, Taquilla Murray, Tiffany Murray, Tyron Murray, Tyelle Murray dec'd, Tamar Murray dec'd. Thomas Sr., died May 22, 2012.

Tanisha Murray, the daughter of Sonya Bartow, and Thomas M. Murray Sr, gave birth to three children; Tymir, Taliha, and Tyrese Murray.

Pauline Evelyn Gumby Sanders married (Harry Pershing Sanders, born October 2, 1917). The couple had the following children; Anna Elizabeth Gumby Krishnappa, Ada Pauline Gumby Richardson, Alvin Harry Gumby Sr., David Neary Sanders, Jeffry Sanders, Lynn Sanders, Debra Kay Sanders, and Frances L. Sanders Williams.

Gumby-Sanders

Debra K. Sanders, the daughter of Pauline and Harry P. Sanders had a son; Jarid E. Sanders (dec'd September 16, 2016).

David N. Sanders, son of Pauline and Harry P. Sanders had a son and one daughter; Andre Brown Sanders, and Tamara Sanders.

Ada Pauline Gumby Richardson, daughter of Pauline and Harry P. Sanders gave birth to two children; Tanecia Richardson, and Tiara Richardson.

Frances Sanders Williams daughter of Pauline and Harry P. Sanders gave birth to two children; Curtis Williams Jr., and Carnella Williams.

Curtis Williams Jr., the son of Frances Sanders Williams had the following children; Courtnee Williams, and Courtland Williams.

Alvin Harry Gumby Sanders Sr., the son of Pauline and Harry P. Sanders had the following children; Altorance Gumby, and Allyn Sanders.

Alvin H. Gumby Jr. had the following children; Charise Gumby Santiago, Emanuel Santiago Gumby, Giovante and Santiago Gumby.

Photo 20 The Anna (William) Gumby family
Seated are Anna E. Courts Gumby, Pauline Gumby Sanders, Charise Gumby Santiago, Alvin Harry Gumby Sanders, Givonte Gumby Santiago.

Photographer – Jeffry Sanders. The picture is courtesy of the John Wesley Gumby Archives

Grandmom

From a very young child, I had fond memories of spending time with my grandmother, Anna Elizabeth Courts Gumby. "Grandmom" is what I affectionately called her when the majority of the other grandchildren called her "Nan Nan." My grandmother taught me so many immeasurable things; how to be sweet, kind, courteous, and respectful. Although she had dozens of grandchildren, she made you feel like you were the "only one" and she exemplified the same level of love with all of us. From the moment, you walked in her door, she tried to feed you and make sure there were not any needs that went unmet. Her furniture was covered with hard plastic, and when you sat down or moved, your every movement made a sound. There were several crystal candy dishes on her coffee table for all to eat. Those dishes were never empty, and she never denied anyone from enjoying sweet treats.

Grandmom was well rounded in all areas, from sports, current news, and the arts. She could be found watching car racing, football, basketball, tennis, ice skating, golfing, square dancing, soap operas, game shows and listening to Soul Train.

Grandmom was not a college graduate, but she encouraged all her children and grandchildren to pursue higher education, and a professional career. As a result, many of her offspring are professionals such as teachers, principals, police officers, medical administrators, and business owners. Many have acquired associates, bachelors, masters and doctoral degrees. My grandmother shared countless hours sharing with me what it was like when the Titanic sank. She shared her experience regarding the Civil Rights movement, the assassination of Medgar Evers, President John F. Kennedy, and Dr. Martin Luther King. She passionately talked about living in the era of "Black only" counters, fountains, restrooms, and sitting in the back of the bus; to be able to sit anywhere, drink from any fountain, and use any restroom she desired. She talked of how she went from riding in a horse and buggy, to a Cadillac. As a result of her struggles, she encouraged me to always do my best! I am who I am today, because she took the time to invest in me emotionally, spiritually, and financially. My grandmother lived to be almost a Century in age. She will forever live in our hearts. Thank you, Grandmom, for investing, believing and nurturing me.

Rev. Dr. Linda M. Baltimore-Green-Gumby

Death Notice John H. Gumby, Saturday April 7, 1900, Page 6

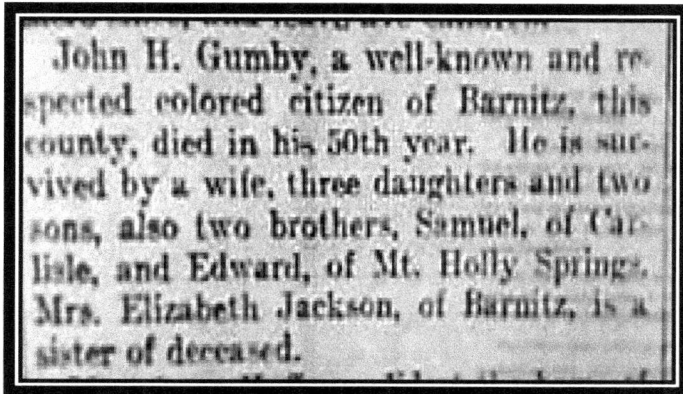

John H. Gumby, a well-known and respected colored citizen of Barnitz, this county, died in his 50th year. He is survived by a wife, three daughters and two sons, also two brothers, Samuel, of Carlisle, and Edward, of Mt. Holly Springs. Mrs. Elizabeth Jackson, of Barnitz, is a sister of deceased.

NEWSPAPER 4 OBITUARY OF JOHN H. GUMBY

Source: Harrisburg Telegraph

The Generations of Harry N. C. Gumby

Harry Nelson Charles Gumby, born April 1, 1892, the son of John Henry Nelson Gumby married Harriet Ann Parker, on December 28, 1916. Harriet Ann Parker was born February 6, 1891. Harriet Ann Parker Gumby was the daughter of Elias Parker and Lucinda Jane Johnson of Mt. Holly Springs, PA.

Slaves freed following the Civil War credited Republican President Abraham Lincoln with their freedom. Like African Americans of the time; Harry Nelson Charles Gumby was a dedicated member of the Republican Party. After President Roosevelt initiated the "New Deal" employment program, African Americans began to affiliate with the Democratic Party. Despite Black support to the democratic party, Harry Nelson Gumby remained a member of the Republican party.

Harry Nelson Charles Gumby worked at a number of jobs to support his household of thirteen family members. Living in a small home, many wondered where the eleven children slept. The home had a small entry hall, and two rooms on the first floor. The second floor contained an entry hall at the top of the stairs, a front bedroom, and a second bedroom. Reportedly, the six brothers slept in the attic. Years later the second floor entry hall was divided into a small bedroom for Harry Nelson's grandson Thomas David Gumby, and afterwards for Harry Nelson's grandson Michael Lynn Gumby.

Harry and Harriet Gumby are buried in the Mount Tabor Cemetery, Mt. Holly Springs, Pennsylvania.

Gravestone of Harry and Harriet Gumby

Photo – Find A Grave

Children of Harry and Harriet Gumby

Photos – Find A Grave

Mary Evelyn Gumby was born October 1, 1912. Mary died May 11, 1985. Mary was the first child born to Harry Nelson and Harriet Ann Parker Gumby.

Raymond Lloyd Gumby was born June 11, 1914. Raymond died February 21, 1990. Raymond is buried in Parklawn Memorial Gardens in Chambersburg, Franklin County, Pennsylvania.

Photo – Find A Grave

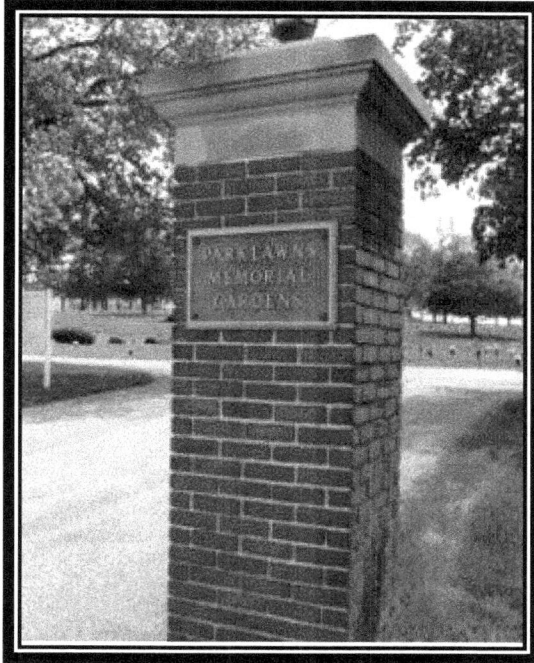

George Henry Gumby was born May 29, 1917. George died May 14, 1939 in Carlisle, Pennsylvania.

NEWSPAPER 5 OBITUARY OF GEORGE H. GUMBY

George H. Gumby, Carlisle, June 23, - George H. Gumby 22, son of Mr. and Mrs. Harry Gumby, Mt. Holly Springs, died Wednesday night at Carlisle Hospital. In addition to his parents, he is survived by five sisters, Mary, Luanda, Ethel, Edna and Harriet, all at home, and five brothers, Raymond, Shippensburg, John Harry, William and Edgar, all of Mt. Holly Springs. Services will be held Sunday at 2. p.m. in West Street A.M.E. Zion Church. Burial will be in Mt. Holly.

Harrisburg PA Telegraph, Friday, June 23, 1939, Page 7

Note: The obituary of George H. Gumby has been reprinted verbatim from the Harrisburg Telegraph News.

Lucinda Jane Gumby

Lucinda Jane Gumby born April 19, 1919, died March 7, 2006.

John Cameron Gumby born November 2, 1921, died June 7, 2004.

Source: Find A Graves

Harry Lester Gumby was born on April 29, 1924. Harry known as "Junie" died July 31, 2014. Harry Jr. is buried with his wife Doris Jean Carroll Gumby in the Forest Hill Cemetery in Kansas City, Missouri.

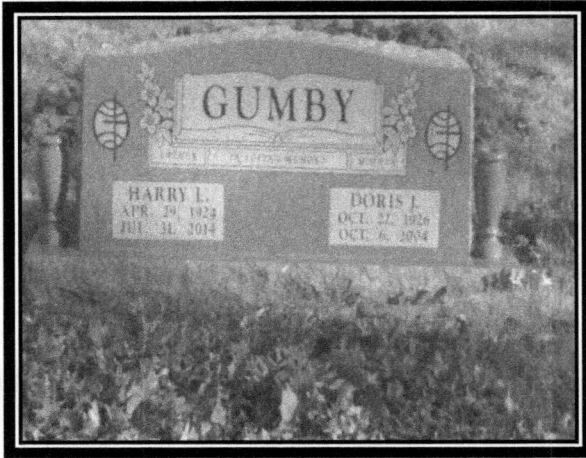

Photo – Courtesy of the Gumby Family

Memories

On Sunday afternoon the Harry Lester Gumby family would assemble around the table for dinner. Two children would sit on each side of the table, and our mother and father at opposite ends of the table. After the food was placed on the table, steaming and hot, our father would get his Bible and would read to us. As hungry kids, we were anxious to say a quick prayer of thanks, and serve our plates to eat. Instead it seemed the Bible scriptures were longer each week!

Once following dinner I asked my father why he read the Bible to us instead of just saying a prayer to bless our food. He told me his father read to his brothers and sisters and his grandfather Gumby did the same with his family. What a legacy!

Rosalind Gumby Bauchum

Edgar Leroy Gumby was born December 15, 1926. Edgar died February 4, 2004. Edgar is buried with his wife Wilhelmina Lofton Gumby in the Brigadier General William C. Doyle Veterans Cemetery in Wrightstown, New Jersey.

Photo – Find A Grave

The living children of Harry Nelson and Harriet Gumby are; Ethel Louise Gumby, born December 15, 1926; Edna Carolyn Gumby, born August 15, 1930; William Lynn Gumby, born September 15, 1933; and his twin sister Harriet Lorene Gumby, born September 15, 1933.

Grandchildren of Harry Nelson and Harriet Gumby

Mary Evelyn Gumby, daughter of Harry Nelson and Harriet Ann Gumby had two children: Loretta Ann Gumby, and Janice M. Gumby. Loretta was born September 11, 1934, and died April 19, 2014.

Janice M. Gumby, the second daughter of Mary Evelyn Gumby was born on April 27, 1936 in Mount Holly Springs PA.

Raymond Lloyd Gumby, son of Harry Nelson and Harriet Ann Gumby married Anna Kaiser Gumby born September 27, 1902. Anna died November 1, 1986. Raymond and Anna through this union had a daughter Frances M. Banks. Frances was born January 29, 1920. (Belvin Carter Banks).

Lucinda Jane Gumby, daughter of Harry Nelson and Harriet Ann Gumby had one son; Thomas David Gumby, born in 1946.

John Cameron Gumby, son of Harry Nelson and Harriet Ann Gumby married Evelyn Gumby born August 31, 1914. John later married Margaret Sellers of Chambersburg PA. There were no children in either union. John Cameron Gumby died June 7, 2004.

Harry Lester Gumby, son of Harry Nelson and Harriet Parker Gumby, married Doris Jean Carroll born October 26, 1926. Doris died October 4, 2004. They had four children;
Brenda Joyce Gumby born in 1947, Harry Bernard Gumby born in 1948, Rosalind Ann Gumby born in 1952, and Arvetta Karen Gumby born in 1953.

Ethel Louise Gumby, daughter of Harry Nelson and Harriet Ann Gumby had one daughter, Tracy Lynn Gumby born in 1965.

Edgar Leroy Gumby, son of Harry Nelson and Harriet Ann Gumby married Wilhelmina Lofton, born February 15, 1923. Edgar died February 19, 2004. Wilhelmina Gumby died June 7, 2009. There were no children to this union.

Edna Carolyn Gumby, daughter of Harry Nelson and Harriet Ann Gumby had one son, Michael Lynn Gumby, born in 1961.

William Lynn Gumby, son of Harry Nelson and Harriet Ann Gumby didn't have children.

Harriet Lorene Gumby, daughter of Harry Nelson and Harriet Ann Gumby didn't have children.

Loretta Ann Gumby, daughter of Mary Evelyn Gumby married Bobby Stanton. Loretta and Bobby Stanton had two children; Alicia Jay Stanton and Lori Jo Stanton. Loretta Gumby Stanton later married John Furman and had one son, Darrell Jay Furman.

Janice Mae Gumby, daughter of Mary Evelyn Gumby married Leon Sweeney. They had the following children: Michael Sweeney[31] and Jacqueline Todd Sweeney. Janice Gumby Sweeney married Jules Ramsey on October 28, 2014.

Thomas David Gumby, son of Lucinda Jane Gumby; had two children; Vanessa Gumby Glass and Tommy Gumby Lebo (No children). Vanessa Gumby Glass had the following children; David Glass, Terrance Glass, Nija Glass and William Glass.

Brenda Joyce Gumby, daughter of Harry L. and Doris Gumby married Bobby Gines in 1968. They had the following children; Millicent Rachel Gines, Brian Eugene Gines, and Jason Elliott Gines.

Harry Bernard Gumby, son of Harry L. and Doris Gumby married Natha Rea Jacobs in 1968. To the union two children were born; Lisa Camille Gumby, and Timothy Erin Gumby.

Harry Gumby later married Juliet Clark Johnson formerly of Jamaica. Two children joined this union. Leroy Johnson (dec'd), and Kimberly Johnson.

Rosalind Ann Gumby, daughter of Harry L. Gumby and Doris Gumby married James William Alexander Bauchum III in 1977. They had the following children: Jessica Ann Bauchum, and Stephanie Lorene Bauchum.

Arvetta Karen Gumby daughter of Harry L. Gumby and Doris Gumby had one son with Frank Bibbs; Marqus Aaron Alphonso Bibbs. Arvetta Gumby later married Thomas Andrew Prewitt. To this union no children were born.

Michael Lynn Gumby, son of Edna Carolyn Gumby married Lisa Boyd. There are not any children to this union.

Tracy Lynn Gumby, daughter of Ethel Louise Gumby married Floyd Cornelius. This union was dissolved. To this union one son was born: Quintin James Cornelius.

Alicia Jay Stanton the daughter of Loretta Gumby Stanton

married Michael T. Thames. The marriage was later dissolved. The couple had one daughter: Jasmine Michelle Thames. Jasmine died in 1994.

Jacqueline Todd Sweeney, daughter of Janice Gumby Sweeney and Leon Sweeney had a daughter, Jennifer L. Sweeney.

Lori Jo Stanton, daughter of Loretta Gumby Furman married Reginald Harris. The marriage was dissolved. They had one daughter, Keri Nicole Harris.

Darrell Jay Furman, son of Loretta Gumby Furman and John Furman married Leslie Furman. They had one daughter Ashley Furman. This marriage was later dissolved.

Leroy Johnson, (dec'd), son of Harry Bernard Gumby and Juliet Gumby had one son, Christian Johnson.

Millicent Gines, daughter of Brenda Joyce Gumby Gines and Bobby Gines married Quint Connor. They had four children; Quint Kevin Connor Jr (dec'd), Kevin Quint Connor, Kyle Austin Connor, and Christopher Isaiah Connor.

Lisa Camille Gumby, daughter of Harry Bernard Gumby and Natha Rea Jacobs married James Trigg. The following children were born: James Trigg Jr., Joshua Ryan Trigg, and Jacob Rylan Trigg. The marriage was later dissolved. Lisa Camille Trigg later married Derrick Williams. Two children joined this union; Aaron and Bianca Williams.

Brian Eugene Gines, son of Brenda Joyce Gumby Gines, and Bobby Eugene Gines, married Michelle Johnigan Gines in 1998. They had three children: Zerryn Gines, Brielle Elise Gines, and Charis Reign Gines.

Timothy Erin Gumby, the son of Harry Bernard Gumby and Natha Rea Jacobs married Stephenae Williams Gumby in 1997. They had the following children: Stephen Gumby, Brooklynn Gumby, and George Gumby.

Jason Elliot Gines, the son of Brenda Joyce Gumby Gines and Bobby Eugene Gines married Kathryn Johnson in 1999. Born to this union were four children: Jason Elliott Gines II, Kyra Simone Gines, Jaden Justice Gines, and Kalia Sanaa Gines.

Kimberly Gumby Johnson, daughter of Harry Bernard Gumby and Juliet Clark Johnson married and had the following children: Charae Lanique Robinson, Gerald Robinson, and Summer Robinson.

Charae Lanique Robinson, daughter of Kimberly Johnson Payne, and the daughter of Juliet (Harry) Gumby gave birth to the following children; Samoria Robinson, and Kamori Robinson.

Chapter 8
Family Photographs

Harry Nelson Charles Gumby was born in Barnitz, PA. When Harry Nelson Charles Gumby was a young boy, his family relocated to Mount Holly Springs Borough, Pennsylvania. During the 1870s former slaves began to settle within the Borough.

PHOTO 21 HARRY NELSON CHARLES GUMBY
Photo courtesy of the Harry N. Gumby Family

Elsie Gumby raised and cared for everyone. Raised in Mount Holly Springs, Elsie moved to Carlisle and resided there for over eight decades.

The youngest child of Rachel Ellen Gumby was Rachel Gumby Arter.

PHOTO 22 ELSIE GUMBY AND RACHEL GUMBY ARTER
Photo courtesy of the Harry N. Gumby Family

Photographs

The following photograph shows Harriet Parker Gumby with her sons, Harry Lester Gumby and Raymond Lloyd Gumby. The three are standing in front of the home first built by Henry Johnson, a former slave from Virginia. The next picture shown is Mary Evelyn Gumby, the first-born daughter of Harry Charles Nelson and Harriet Gumby.

PHOTO 23 HARRY, HARRIET, RAYMOND, AND MARY GUMBY
Photo courtesy of the Harry N. Gumby Family

Mary, Loretta, and Janice Gumby

PHOTO 24 MARY GUMBY AND DAUGHTERS
Photos courtesy of the Harry N. Gumby Family

LUCINDA, HARRY, AND JOHN CAMERON GUMBY

PHOTO 25 LUCINDA J., JOHN C., AND HARRY L. GUMBY

Photos courtesy of the Harry N. Gumby Family

Ethel Louise Gumby, life-long resident of Mount Holly Springs was an active member in the community. Ethel was recognized by the Pennsylvania Voter Hall of Fame for fifty consecutive years of voting. (Ridge Administration Inducts 73 Cumberland County Residents Into State Voter Hall of Fame)

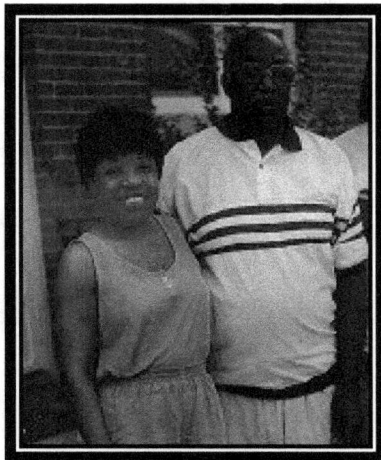

Courtesy of the Harry NelsonGumby Family

William Lynn Gumby, the first family member to receive a degree in the biological and chemical sciences from Dickinson College, Carlisle, PA.

Photo 26 William, Harriet, Gumby
Photos courtesy of the Harry N. Gumby Family

PHOTO 27 EDNA GUMBY

Edna Carolyn Gumby, a faithful servant of the Shiloh Baptist Church. Edna served in the Usher Ministry for over fifty years.

Photos courtesy of the Harry N. Gumby Family

The Epilogue

I am truly blessed and thankful for my cousin Rosalind Gumby Bauchum. Her outstanding research tracing our family history from the 1700s to the present is a great achievement.

The Gumby family thanks her for her hard work, perseverance, strength, and uplifting spirit; as this family moves forward in the years to come. May God continue to bless you and yours.

Much Love,
John W. Gumby Sr. PhD

From row. Arvetta Gumby Prewitt, Doris Carroll Gumby, Mother
Second row. Rosalind Gumby Bauchum, Harry Bernard Gumby
Brenda Gumby Gines.

PHOTO 28 DORIS J. GUMBY AND CHILDREN
Photo courtesy of the Harry N. Gumby Family

LIST OF DOCUMENTS

DOCUMENT 1. NELSON GUMBY AS A FREE MAN......................................25

DOCUMENT 2. 1860 WARREN, VIRGINIA CENSUS...........................27

DOCUMENT 3, 1870 CUMBERLAND COUNTY CENSUS 30

DOCUMENT 4 ENTRY OF JOHN GUMBY'S BAPTISM...............................33

DOCUMENT 5. WILLIAM GUMBY USCT.....................................42

DOCUMENT 6. NOAH GUMBY ENLISTMENT...43

DOCUMENT 7. WILLIAM H. GUMBY DRAFT CARD.............................45

DOCUMENT 8. WAR CARD OF GEORGE W. GUMBY 47

DOCUMENT 9. PRESIDENTIAL SERVICE AWARD 50

DOCUMENT 10. NELSON GUMBY'S FREE REGISTRATION PAPER.........80

DOCUMENT 11. MARRIAGE APPLICATION FOR CHARLES EDWARD
     AND MARY EMMA BOWERS 81

DOCUMENT 12 - 1940 PENNSYLVANIA CENSUS 90

LIST OF NEWSPAPER ARTICLES

NEWSPAPER 1 CHARLES EDWARD GUMBY 79

NEWSPAPER 2 OBITUARY OF SAMUEL GUMBY 83

NEWSPAPER 3 OBITUARY OF ANNA GUMBY 84

NEWSPAPER 4 OBITUARY OF JOHN H. GUMBY 105

NEWSPAPER 5 OBITUARY OF GEORGE H. GUMBY 110

LIST OF PHOTOGRAPHS

PHOTO 1. TOM AND KATE GUMBY 4

PHOTO 2 JOHN CARTER - PHOTO – WIKIPEDIA 7

PHOTO 3 ROBERT KING CARTER.. 10

PHOTO 4. NOMINI HALL.. 12

PHOTO 5 ROBERT CARTER III 16

 PHOTO 6 GUMBY FAMILY HISTORY NOTES 20

PHOTO 7. THE MOUNT TABOR AMEZ CHURCH PARSONAGE 31

PHOTO 8 A VIRGINIA SLAVE CABIN.. 34

PHOTO 9 MOUNT TABOR AFRICAN METHODIST EPISCOPAL ZION
        CHURCH 36

PHOTO 10. WEST STREET AME ZION CHURCH........................ 38

PHOTO 11 HARRY GUMBY REGISTRATION 46

PHOTO 12 HENRY SPRADLEY 54

PHOTO 13. GUMBY'S BARBERSHOP.. 55

PHOTO 14. PURPOSE PUBLISHING COMPANY 56

PHOTO 15. EDGAR GUMBY SINGS 63

PHOTO 16. SHILOH BAPTIST OF CARLISLE PA 67

PHOTO 17. BAUCHUM SISTERS MUSIC...................................... 68

PHOTO 18. MOUNT TABOR CEMETERY 70

PHOTO 19 SONS AND GRANDSON OF WILLIAM H. GUMBY................ 101

PHOTO 20 THE ANNA (WILLIAM) GUMBY FAMILY 103

PHOTO 21 HARRY NELSON CHARLES GUMBY 119

PHOTO 22 ELSIE GUMBY AND RACHEL GUMBY ARTER..... 120

PHOTO 23 HARRY, HARRIET, RAYMOND, AND MARY GUMBY........... 121

PHOTO 24 MARY GUMBY AND DAUGHTERS 122

PHOTO 25 LUCINDA J., JOHN C., AND HARRY L. GUMBY..... 123

PHOTO 26 WILLIAM, HARRIET, GUMBY 125

PHOTO 27 EDNA GUMBY.. 126

PHOTO 28 DORIS J. GUMBY AND CHILDREN 128

Works Cited

1850-1880, U.S. Census Mortality Schedules -. "Ancestry.com." 31 May
    1880. 16 February 2016. <ancestry.com>.

Administration, National Archives and Records. "Electronic Army Serial
    Number Merged File, ca. 1938 - 1946 ." 01 - 30 June - September
    2002. *National Archives and Records Administraiton.* 20 October
    2013.
    <http://research.archives.gov/description/1263923/06311.148>.

Administration, National Archives. "Compiled Military Service Records of
    Volunteer Union Soldiers Who Served the United States Colored
    Troops: Miscellaneous Cards." 1 March 2013. *Fold 3.* 15 March
    2016.
    <https://www.fold3.com/image/307183302/?terms=Gumby>.

Arnett, John. "Barbados." 1998. *Summary of some Barbados Records of
    Arnett Families.* 29 January 2016. <http://www.chbc-
    lky.org/arnettforest/barbados.htm>.

"Barbados.Org." 1995-2015. *The History of Barbados; 1644-1700 Slavery
    and Sugar.* 30 January 2016.
    <http://www.barbados.org/history1.htm#.Vq1MgfkrLIU>.

Bauchum, Rosalind Gumby. "Listing of African Americans in Mt. Holly
    Springs PA in 1900." Bauchum, Rosalind Gumby. *Elias and Lucinda
    Parker, The Case for a Civil War Widow's Pension.* Mount Holly
    Springs: Purpose Publishing Company, Missouri, 2011. 58-63.

Bauchum, Rosalind. "The Pension Papers." Bauchum, Rosalind G. *Elias and
    Lucinda Parker; The Case for a Civil War Widow's Pension.*
    Grandview: Purpose Publishing, 2012. 68.

Bitts-Jackson, Mary Alice. "Intertwining Journeys, Family and College
    Histories Come Full Circle." *Dickinson (Dickinson College)* (2013).

Bookwalter, Judy. "History of Cumberlandand Adam Counties, PA." 2009.
    Genweb. 3 December 2013.
    <http://files.usgwarchives.net/pa/cumberland/history/local/beers
    1886/beers-35.txt>.

Cards, United States World War I Draft Registration. "United States World War I Draft Registration Cards." 1917 - 1918. *Family Search.* 04 July 2014. <https://familysearch.org/pal:MM9.1.1/K6VH-LRB:>.

Carson, Jane. "Plantation Housekeeping in Colonial Virginia." 1974.

"Carter Papers." *The Virginia Magazine of History and Biography, Volume 6, No 1* (1898): 12.

Census, 1810 United States Virginia. "www.freeafricanamericans.com/1810VAa.htm ." 1810. *Free African-Americans.com.* 2013.

Census, 1860 US Federal. "United States Census, 1860, index,." 2014. *Family Search.* <https://familysearch.org/pal:MM9.1.1/M41N-7L7:>.

Census, 1940. *FamilySearch, Ronald Owens in the household of Rachel E. Gumby.* 1940. 28 October 2015. <https://familysearch.org/ark:/61903/1:1:KQHX-1TJ>.

Commons, WikiMedia. *File Map, US Slave/Free (States) 1789.* 14 October 2010. 24 September 2015. <https://commons.wikimedia.org/wiki/File:US_SlaveFree1789.gif>.

Database, People Search. *Gumby (last name) in the US Identify People Search Database .* 10 May 2013. www.usidentity.com/1/gumby. 10 May 2013.

"Diary, Correspondence and Papers of Robert Carter 1702-1732, Collection transcribed by Edmund Berkely, Jr." n.d. *University of Virginia Library.* 30 October 2014. <http://carter.lib.virginia.edu/html/cd1723.html#n32>.

"Diary, Correspondence and Papers of Robert Carter 1702-1732, Collection transcribed by Edmund Berkely, Jr." n.d. *University of Virginia Library.* 30 October 2014. <http://carter.lib.virginia.edu/html/cd1723.html#n32>.

Donald E. Owens, Sr. *Gardner Library Stories, Donald E. Owens, Sr.* Rachael Zuck. 11 August 2005. http://gardnerlibrary.org/stories/donald-e-owens-sr. 17 November 2016.

Douthat, Robert. "1840 Warren County, Virginia Census." *1840 Warren County Virginia Census*. Signal, TN: Mountain Press, 2000. 36 .

Emory University, National Endowment for the Humanitites, W.E.B. Institute, Harvard University. *African Origens: Portal to Africans Liberated from Transatlantic* . 2009. 15 February 2016. <www.african-origins.org>.

Farris, Patrick. "Slavery in Front Royal was different from that in Tidewater." *The Northern Virginia Daily* 27 February 2013: 1. News article.

Fithian, Philip Vickers. "A Plantation Tutor of the Old Dominion, 1773-1774." Fithian, Philip Vickers. *Journal and Letters of Philip Vickers Fithian: A Plantation Tutor of the Old Dominion: 1773-1774*. n.d.

Genealogy, Binns. "1790 /1800 Virginia Tax List Census." 2008, 2010. *Binns Genealogy*. 21 September 2014. <http://www.binnsgenealogy.com/VirginiaTaxListCensuses/Frederick/>.

"Genealogy; from Stafford County, Virginia Deeds and Wills, 1699-1709." n.d. *http://www.werelate.org/wiki/Person:Sarah_Foote_(32)*. 12 November 2014. <http://www.werelate.org/wiki/Person:Sarah_Foote_(32)>.

Hast, Adele. "The Legal Status of the Negro in Virginia 1705-1765." *Journal of Negro History, Volume 54, Number 3* (1969): 228.

Heinegg, Paul. "Free African Americans of Virginia, North Carolina, South Carolina, Maryland and Delaware." n.d. *freeafricanamericans.com*. 2013. <http://www.usu.edu/history/faculty/nicholls/manumissions/index.htm >.

—. "Free African-Americans of North Carolina, Virginia and South Carolina; From the Colonial Period to 1820." 2005. *Free African-Americans.com*. 10 November 2014. <http://www.freeafricanamericans.com/East_Indians.htm Martha Gumby/>.

—. "Westmoreland County Personal Property Tax List, 1782 - 1815." 1782. *http://www.freeafricanamericans.com/westtax.htm.* 18 January 2015. <http://www.freeafricanamericans.com/westtax.htm>.

Hill, Samuel. Hill, Samuel. *Varieties of Southern Religious Experience.* Louisiana State University Press, 1988.

"Information about Sarah Foote (32) Genealogy." 1704. *Werelate.org.* 12 November 2014. <http://www.werelate.org/wiki/Person:Sarah_Foote_(32)>.

"Inward Slave Manifest for the Port of New Orleans." n.d.

Jr., Digitized by Edmund Berkeley. "The Diary Correspondence and Papers of Robert King Carter of Virginia." 16 October 1732. *Library of Virginia.* 6 December 2014. <http://carter.lib.virginia.edu/html/RCwill.html>.

Legacy, Nominy Hall Slave. "Nominy Hall Slave Legacy." n.d. *Nominy Hall Slave Legacy; History of the Carter Family.* 29 January 2015. <http://nominihallslavelegacy.com/history-of-the-carter-family>.

"Library of Virginia Archives." October 10 1727. *www.upress.virginia.edu/plunkett/PluAfro.all.* 21 November 2016.

MacDonald, Joy. "Free Blacks in Frederick County, VA, Tax Records 1793-1862." 2009.

McCartney, Martha. *Encylopedia Virginia, Publication of Virginia Foundation for the Humanities.* 29 August 2011. 18 February 2016. <http://www.encyclopediavirginia.org/virginia_s_first_africans>.

Monaghan, E. Jennifer. "New Paths to Literacy Acquisition ." Monaghan, E. Jennifer. *Learning to Read and Write in Colonial America.* Amherst: University of Massachusetts Press, 2005. 342.

National Society of the Colonial Dames of America in the Commonwealth of Virginia. Parish Register of Christ Church, Middlesex County, Virginia from 1653 to 1812. *Ancestry.com; Christ Church Parish, Virginia Births, 1653-1812 [database on-line].* . 1897. 22 June 2016. <http://www.ancestry.com/>.

Onstott, Philip. "The Tribes of Western Africa; Senegal to Angola." Onstott, Philip. *The Tribes of Western Africa; Senegal to Angola*. Berkeley, CA: University of California, Berkeley, 2015. 510.

Owens, Donald. *The Escape to Freedom* Rosalind Gumby Bauchum. April 2014.

"Pennsylvania Marriages, 1709-1940," (https://familysearch.org/ark:/61903/1:1:V26Z-4YL :." 1899 November 1899. *FamilySearch.* 23 February 2016. <https://familysearch.org >.

"Pennsylvania, County Marriages, 1885-1950, data base with images." 24 June 2016. *FamilySearch (https://familysearch.org/ark:/61903/1:1:VFS4-43N* . 1 October 2016. <Https://familysearch.org >.

R. L. Polk and Company, Compilers. R. L. Polk and Company, Compilers. *Boyd's Harrisburg Directory*. Harrisburg, PA: R. L. Polk and Company, Compilers, 1926.

Randall, Philip Gorden and Geneva Christensen. Randall, Philip Gorden and Geneva Christensen. *Fire in their Bones, The True Story of a Missionary Couple's Forty years in Africa*. Eugene, OR: WIPF & Stock, 2008. 95.

"Ridge Administration Inducts 73 Cumberland County Residents Into State Voter Hall of Fame." *PR Newswire* 17 October 2000: 1.

Rockland, slave quarters, Leesburg, Loudoun County, Virginia. n.d.

Rutman, Darrett B and Anita Rutman. "http://archiver.rootsweb.ancestry.com/th/read/SLAVEINFO/200 0-04/0957121472 ." April 2000. *Rootsweb.Ancestry.com.* 15 October 2014. <http://archiver.rootsweb.ancestry.com/th/read/SLAVEINFO/200 0-04/0957121472 >.

Search, Family. " Pennsylvania Marriages 1885-1950, Charles E. Gumby and Mary C. Bowers." 06 January 1898. *Family Search.* 04 July 2014. <https://familysearch.org/pal:/MM9.1.1/VFW8-G83>.

Sigmund, Luther J. "Death of Henry WI Spradley." *The Dickinson* (1897): Issue 24, Page 1.

Society, Allen County Public Library and the Virginia Historical. "Carter Papers; Will of Robert King Carter, June 1730." *Virginia History Magazine* June 1899.

Society, Virginia Historical. *Slave Owners, Westmoreland County, VA 1782*. January 1902. 16 July 2015. <http://www.jstor.org/stable/4242527>.

—. *Virginia Historical Society*. 1773. 1 February 2015. <http://www.vahistorical.org>.

Stewart, Nancy B. "How did Shenandoah County get into the slavery business?" (n.d.): 9.

Taylor, Frances Henle. "www.rivahresearch.com/westmorelandcty/westmorelandcounty.htm." 18 June 2007. *Westmoreland County Rootsweb*. 15 March 2014. <http://www.rivahresearch.com/westmorelandcty/westmorelandcounty.htm>.

"The Corotoman Slave Histories." 14 May 1655. *Christ Church 1735*. 5 November 2016. <https://christchurch1735.knack.com>.

United States Census, 1870. "Family Search.org." n.d. *Family Search*. 04 July 2014. <https://familysearch.org/pal:MM9.1.1/MZGX-NYT>.

"United States Census, 1930, database with images." 8 December 2016. *Familysearch.org*. 4 October 2016. <https://familysearch.org/ark:/61903/1:1:XHSS-VDH>.

United States Census, 1980. "Family Search." n.d. *Family Search*. 14 September 2014. <https://familysearch.org/pal:MM9.1.1MWFM-KQX:>.

"United States, GenealogyBank Obituaries, 1980-2014." 10 September 2016. *FamilySearch (https://familysearch.org/ark:/61903/1:1:QV58-ZJ27, database with images,*. 1 October 2016. <https://familysearch.org/ark:/61903/1:1:QV58-ZJ27>.

"United States, GenealogyBank Obituaries, 1980-2014," database with images." 2016 September 2016.

https://familysearch.org/ark:/61903/1:1:QVT2-3LVF. 1 October
2016. <https://familysearch.org/ark:/61903/1:1:QVT2-3LVF>.

Washington DC: National Archives and Records Administration, n.d.
"United States Census 1830." 1830. *Family Search.* January 25
January 2016. <https://familysearch.org/pal:/MM9.3.1/TH-1951-
25139-19813-26?cc=1803958>.

"Westmoreland County Records and Inventories, 1767 - 1776." n.d.
www.gunstonhall.org/library/probate/NEWTON67.PDF. 13
January 2015.
<www.gunstonhall.org/library/probate/NEWTON67.PDF>.

Westmoreland County, VA Records and Inventories. "Newton67.PDF." 28
July 1767. *Newton67.PDF.* 29 December 2014.
<http://www.Gunstonhall.org>.

"Whites and Blacks living at Nomony Hall in Westmoreland County, 1775."
Westmoreland County, VA: Collections from the Virginia Historical
Society, 25 August 1775.

Books by the Author

1. Bauchum, Rosalind Gumby, *The Story of Gumby; Tracing Family History to the 1700s*, (Grandview MO: Purpose Publishing Company, 2015)

2. Bauchum, Rosalind Gumby, *Elias and Lucinda Parker; the Quest for a Civil War Widow's Pension,* (Grandview MO: Purpose Publishing Company, 2012)

3. Bauchum, Rosalind Gumby, *African-American Organizations: 1794-1999, A Selected Bibliography Sourcebook,* (Lanham Maryland, New York, Oxford, England: University Press of America 2001)

4. Bauchum, Rosalind G., *The Black Business and Professional Woman; Selective References of Achievement,* (Monticello, IL: Vance Bibliographies, 1985)

5. Bauchum, Rosalind Gumby, *Needs Assessment Methodologies in the Development of Impact Statements,* (Monticello, IL: Vance Bibliographies, 1985)

6. Bauchum, Rosalind G., *Economics of Health Maintenance Organizations; A Bibliography,* (Monticello, IL: Vance Bibliographies, 1984)

7. Bauchum, Rosalind G., *Health Planning for the Elderly; A Selected and Partially Annotated Bibliography,* (Monticello, IL: Vance Bibliographies, 1984)

8. Bauchum, Rosalind G., *Social Planning in Urban Planning,* Chicago, IL: Council of Planning Librarians, 1983)

9. Bauchum, Rosalind G., *St. Peter Lutheran Church and the Citi Corp Center, Mixed Use Designing in Urban Architecture,* (Monticello, IL: Vance Bibliographies, 1983)

10. Bauchum, Rosalind G., *The Black Architect,* (Monticello IL: Vance Bibliographies, 1982)

11. Bauchum, Rosalind G. *Introduction to Project Planning and Management for Public Organizations, Selected References* (Monticello IL: Vance Bibliographies, 1981)

12. Bauchum, Rosalind G., *New Concepts in Hotel and Convention Center Designs,* (Monticello, IL: Vance Bibliographies, 1982)

13. Bauchum, Rosalind G. *New Trends in Condominium and Cooperative Conversions; Annotated Bibliography,* (Monticello, IL: Vance Bibliographies, 1982)

14. Bauchum, Rosalind G., *Landscaping in Downtown Revitalized Areas,* Monticello IL: Vance Bibliographies, 1982)

15. Bauchum, Rosalind G., *Industrial Development of Urban Space, Land-Use planning for Central City Development, A Selected and Annotated Bibliography,* (Chicago IL: Council of Planning Librarians, 1982)

16. Bauchum, Rosalind G., *Cluster Housing, Theory, Design, Perceptions on Cluster Density, and an Annotated Bibliography,* (Monticello, IL: Vance Bibliographies, 1982)

17. Bauchum, Rosalind G., *Planning; a Bibliography of selected urban, environmental, social, transportation, Land-use, program and general planning references.* (Grandview, MO: Rosalind Bauchum, Self-Published, 1983)

18. Bauchum, Rosalind G., *Land-use, program and general planning references.* (Grandview, MO: Rosalind Bauchum, Self-Published, 1983)

19. Bauchum, Rosalind G., *Proposal Development and Project Planning Sourcebook,* R. G. Bauchum and Associates, Inc. 1982

20. Bauchum, Rosalind G. *Project management for neighborhood rehabilitation and revitalization projects: a selected bibliography.* (Monticello, IL: Vance Bibliographies, 1982)

End notes

[1] The Project Gutenberg EBook of Journal and Letters of Philip Vickers. Fithian: A Plantation Tutor of the Old Dominion, 1773-1774., by Philip Vickers Fithian, Title: Journal and Letters of Philip Vickers Fithian: A Plantation Tutor of the Old Dominion, 1773-1774, www.gutenberg.org.
[2] The Corotoman Slave History project conducted by Dr. Patrick Heffernan researched early documents associated with Corotoman Plantation.
[3] Inward Slave Manifests for the Port of New Orleans Roll 12, 1837-1839.
[4] Stewart, Nancy B. How did Shenandoah County get into the slavery business? Page 9
[5] Hill, Samuel. Hill, Samuel. *Varieties of Southern Religious Experience.* Louisiana State University Press, 1988.

[6] Deed of Emancipation, Nomoni Hall Slave Legacy Project - freed 509 slaves, http://nominihallslavelegacy.com/the-deed-of-gift/, Filed in Northumberland County, Virginia, September 5, 1791
[7] Michael Nicholls and Lenaye Howard of Utah State University abstracted the deeds and wills for Dinwiddie, Prince George, Chesterfield, Charles City, Isle of Wight, Southampton, Surry, and Sussex Counties. (Heinegg, Free African Americans of Virginia, North Carolina, South Carolina, Maryland and Delaware)
[8] p.244, I Robert Carter set free Sarah Brutus, Judith Brutus, Abby Gumby, Sampson Robinson, James Robinson, Charlotte Newman, Dinah Richards, and Aggy Robinson. 2 January 1792
[99] Virginia Slaves Freed After 1782 Westmoreland County, Virginia. Compiled and abstracted from various web research including Deeds, Wills & Court Orders for the Westmoreland County Rootsweb site, (Taylor) (Carson) (MacDonald)htm by Francesca Henle Taylor, historybuff@rivahresearch.com Completed: June 18, 2007
[10] Carson, Jane, Plantation Housekeeping in Colonial Virginia, (1974) Colonial Williamsburg Foundation Library Research Report Series - RR0136, Colonial Williamsburg Foundation, Williamsburg, Virginia 1990

[12] "Other Free" Heads of Household in the 1810 Virginia Census, by Family Name

(Microfilm M252, reels 66-71)

http://www.freeafricanamericans.com/1810VAa.htm

Gumby, John 9 p.562 Frederick County

Gumby, Rachel 5 p.595 Frederick County

[13] Douthat, Robert, 1840 Warren County, Virginia Census Mountain Press, Signal TN

[14] Robert Carter III of Nomini Hall, 1753, Thomas Hudson (1701–1779) Oil on canvas

[15]Gift of Louise Anderson Patten, 1972.17, Source Wikipedia, http://en.wikipedia.org/wiki/Robert_Carter_III, accessed, October 27, 2014

[15] Index to the List of Free Negroes Offered for Hire for taxes and levies at DEC Court; 1851, Frederick County Virginia Free Negro and Slave Records, 1795-1871, Library of Virginia, 1117610 0003 0002, Accessed by R. Bauchum, December 1, 2016

[16] "United States Census, 1860", database with images, *FamilySearch* (https://familysearch.org/ark:/61903/1:1:M41B-F9V: 30 December 2015), James Gumbie in entry for Jas Grubbs, 1860.

[17] Story passed down through generations and told to Donald Owens, grandson of Elsie Gumby.

[18] "United States Census, 1880," database with images, *FamilySearch* (https://familysearch.org/ark:/61903/1:1: MWVZ-3HN: accessed 2 September 2015), John H Gumby in household of George K Binkley, Orwigsburgh, Schuylkill, Pennsylvania, United States; citing enumeration district 243, sheet 260A, NARA microfilm publication T9 (Washington D.C.: National Archives and Records Administration, n.d.), roll 1194; FHL microfilm 1,255,194.

[19] Bookwalter, Judy, History of Cumberland, and Adam Counties Pennsylvania, A historical review first published in 1886. Section XXV, pages 347-376, Borough of Mount Holly Springs, http://www.usgwarchives.net/pa/cumberland/beers/beers.htm

[20] West Street AMEZ Church, Harrisburg AMEZ District, http://www.harrisburgdistrictamez.com/West-Street-AME-Zion-Church.html accessed April 10, 2016 by Rosalind G. Bauchum.

[21] Internet (Cards)

[22] Gumby Family in Professions and Business. This section is based upon information provided by Gumby Family individuals. Gumby names not displayed within a category were not submitted prior to publication.

23 Carter.lib.virginia.edu/html/cd1723.html#n32 (Diary, Correspondence and Papers of Robert Carter 1702-1732, Collection transcribed by Edmund Berkely, Jr.)
24 "Papers of Robert 'King' Carter of ' Corotoman,' Lancaster County, Va.," Mss1 C2468 a 10, Virginia Historical Society, Richmond http://carter.lib.virginia.edu/html/C33slaves.html, accessed November 12, 2014.
25 Barden, John Randolph., PhD, "Flushed with notions of freedom: The growth and emancipation of a Virginia slave community, 1732-1812." Duke University, 1993, 733 pages, 9416895
26 IBID
27 1850 Federal Census, House 809, Family number 820, Line 33, M432 affiliate publication 980, GS Film 444970, Digital folder 004206470
28 Cody, Cheryll Ann, Slave names and naming in Barbados 1650-1830 in Jerome S. Handler and JoAnn Jacoby, *The William and Mary Quarterly*, Vol. 53, No. 4 (Oct., 1996), pp. 685-728 Note: Cody conducted a study of the Ball Plantation in South Carolina as cited on page 687.
29 "Pennsylvania, County Marriages, 1885-1950," index and images, www.familysearch.com (https://familysearch.org/pal:/MM9.1.1/VFW8-G83: accessed 04 Jul 2014), Charles E. Gumby and Mary C. Bowers, 06 Jan 1898; (Search)citing, Cumberland, Pennsylvania, United States; FHL microfilm 21009.
30 Pennsylvania, County Marriages, 1885-1950", database with images, *FamilySearch* (https://familysearch.org/ark:/61903/1:1:KHNZ-FZF: 24 June 2016), Sarah Jane Greason in entry for Chester Ray James and Annabell Prunty, 1923

INDEX

A

Amos Gumby · 40

B

Bauchum

Index

Jessica A. · 68

Stephanie Lorene · 68

C

Careers

   Gumby Family · 55

   Gumby's Barber Shop · 57

Carlisle

   DickinsonCollege · 53

Carter

   Deed of Gift · 13

   Robert III · iv

Carter Manumission · 13

Counties

   Frederick · 17

   Northumberland · 13

   Shenandoah · 11

   Warren · 17

   Westmoreland · 13

Cumberland County, PA

   Colored School · 34

Curtis

   Robert · 92

D

Dickinson College

   Esther Popel Shaw · 54

E

Education · 57, 62

F

Fithian · 3

Front Royal · 20

G

Gumby · 3, 6, 11

   Abby · 74

   Alice · 92

   Alvin Harry Sr. · 102

   Angela D · 68

   Anna · 84

   Annie Elizabeth Courts · 97

   Arvetta Karen · 115, 116

   Betty Anna Krishnappa · 64, 102

   Brenda Joyce · 115, 116, 118

   Charles E. · 81

   Charles Edward · 78

   Clouden · 74

   Dadda · 3

   Dadda (Tom) · 11

   Danielle Ashe · 68

   Dorcas · 74

   Edgar Leroy · 113

   Edna Carolyn · 113, 115, 126

   Elijah · 77, 78

   Elsie M. · 87

   Ethel Louise · 113

   Ethel Louise Gumby · 124

   Evaline · 78

   Evelyn · 115

   Frances · 74

   George Henry · 110

Gumbee · 11

Harriet Lorene · 113, 115, 125

Harriet Lorene Gumby · 125

Harry Bernard · 115, 116

Harry Lester · 36, 112, 115

Harry Nelson Charles · 44, 106

Humphrey · 74

Jack · 71, 73

Jacob · 78

James · 78

Jane · 92

Janice M. · 114

Janice Mae · 116

Janice Sweeney Ramsey · 19

Joan · 74

John · 13, 17, 62, 74, 86, 89

John Cameron · 111, 115

John H. · 33

John Henry Nelson · 78

John W. Sr. · 127

John Wesley · 64, 97

Kate · 72

Katy · 73

Loretta Ann · 114

Loretta Furman · 19

Lucinda Jane · 111

Margaret Sellers · 115

Mary · 78

Mary Evelyn · 108

Michael Lynn · 117

Nelson · 13, 16, 19, 22, 29, 32, 73, 74, 78, 80, 81, 85, 92, 119

Ngombe · 5

Pauline E. · 97

Rachel · 7, 17, 73, 75, 89

Rachel Ellen Sims · 85

Raymond Lloyd · 109, 121

Richard Lester · 98

Robert Walter · 99

Rosalind Ann · 116

Rosalind Bauchum · 63, 127

Samboe · 75

Samuel · 82, 83

Samuel D. · 78

Sarah · 74

Story of Escape to Barnitz PA · 32

Thomas · 74, 75

Thomas David · 114

Tom (Dadda) · 71

Tommy Lebo · 116

Tracy Lynn · 117

Vivian Anna · 97

Wilhelmina Lofton · 115

William Henry · 99

William Henry Jr. · 97

William Henry Sr. · 97

William L. · 61

William Lynn · 113, 115, 125

Willoughby/Willoby · 74

Gumby Richardson

    Ada Pauline Richardson · 102

Gumby's Barber Shop · 55

H

Harry Charles Nelson Gumby · 46

Heinegg

    Paul · 7

L

Law enforcement · 59

M

MAGIC
  Midwest Afro American Genealogy
    Interest Coalition · iii
Manumission
  Gift of Deed · 13
Miles
  Jeanette Richard · iii
  Rev. John Modest · iii
Military Service · 59
Mount Holly Springs · 32, 53
  Mount Tabor · 29, 35, 69, 86, 106

N

Negroes · 3
Nelson · *See* Gumby
Nomini Hall · iv

P

Parker
  Elias Van Buren · 67
Pennsylvania
  Barnitz · 86
  Barnitz · 29, 32
  Barnitz · 119
Professional Careers · 60

R

Robert Carter · 13
Robert King Carter · 8, 12, 17, 72

S

Ships
  Barque Hortensia · 11
  Empressa, Jacuhy · 5
Slaves
  James Gumby, slave owner · 11
  Mason-Dixon Line · 32
  Treatment · 17
St. Paul's Evangelical Lutheran · 33

T

Tom (Dadda) Gumby · 12

U

United States Colored Troops
  General Order 329 · 39
US Colored Troops
  Anthony Gumby · 40
  Jacob Gumby · 40
  Jeremiah Gumby · 40
  John Gumby · 40
  Lewis Gumby · 40
  Noah Gumby · 40
  Noel Gumby · 40
  William Gumby · 40

V

Virginia · 19
   Carter Family · 13

W

Wars

Story of Gumby
   World War I · 44
   World War II · 46
Westmoreland County · iv
**William Henry Gumby's World
   War I Registration**
   Gumby · 45

About the Author

Rosalind Gumby Bauchum is an author, and researcher. Rosalind's latest book captures her enjoyment of genealogical history and research.

In addition to this book, "The Story of Gumby; Tracing Family History to the 1700s," other history-related titles include; African-American Organizations; 1794 – 1999; "The Black Architect," Elias and Lucinda Parker; the case for a Civil War Widow's Pension, and The Black Business and Professional Woman: Selected References of Achievement. Rosalind's interest in public administration, urban planning, community development, and neighborhood revitalization are topics in thirteen additional publications.

Rosalind earned a bachelor's degree in Human Development and Family Life (Child Development - Applied Behavior Science), and a Master of Public Administration (MPA) degree from the University of Kansas.

Rosalind worked in the health and human services, organization and business services, and the Federal Civil Service. Rosalind has two adult children, Jessica and Stephanie, and lives in the Midwest with her husband James.

Rosalind is a member of the Midwest Afro American Genealogy Interest Coalition (MAGIC), the Association for the Study of African-American Life and History, Kansas City Study Group, and the Northern Neck of Virginia Historical Society. Rosalind also holds memberships in Alpha Kappa Alpha Sorority, Inc., the Kansas University Alumni Association, KU Black Alumni Network. and the Greater Kansas City Chapter of the National Association of Negro Business and Professional Women's Clubs Inc.

www.ingramcontent.com/pod-product-compliance
Lightning Source LLC
Chambersburg PA
CBHW072136020426
42334CB00018B/1827